CANOE TRIP

CANOE TRIP

ALONE IN THE MAINE WILDERNESS

DAVID CURRAN

HELLGATE PRESS   ASHLAND, OREGON

Hellgate Press
PO Box 3531
Ashland, OR 97520

email: info@hellgatepress.com

First edition originally published by Stackpole Books, 2002. This edition is published and printed, with permission, by Hellgate Press, an imprint of L&R Publishing, LLC.

Original cover design by Caroline Stover
Cover photo by David Curran
Cover modifications by L. Redding

Library of Congress Cataloging-in-Publication Data
Curran, David K., 1951-
   Canoe trip : alone in the Maine wilderness / David Curran. -- 2nd ed.
      p. cm.
   ISBN 978-1-55571-673-8
   1. Canoes and canoeing--Maine--Allagash River. 2. Curran, David K., 1951---Travel--Maine--Allagash River. I. Title.
   GV782.42.C87C87 2010
   917.41'1--dc22
                                                    2010028821

Printed and bound in the United States of America

Second edition 10 9 8 7 6 5 4 3 2

FOR KEVIN AND MARIAH

ACKNOWLEDGMENTS

I HAVE BEEN, THROUGHOUT MY LIFE, THE GRATEFUL RECIPIENT OF A great deal of good luck, an essential element in any sort of undertaking. The reader will doubtless note many examples of it in the pages to follow. Good fortune has certainly played a role in the publication of this book. I was fortunate to have my manuscript land on the desk of an editor, Judith Schnell, who happens to be from Maine and whose grandfather happens to have been a river man, a log driver no less. I was lucky to have crossed paths with Walter Bickford who got my mind right about the ideal of wilderness travel and steered me to Maine. I was lucky to have known two readers, Kevin Rose and Amanda Waldron, who took the time to go over the manuscript and give me their honest opinion of its faults and merits. Finally, I have been lucky to be married to Pat, who has not only been excited to see me leave but quite pleased to have me return.

AUTHOR'S NOTE

THIS BOOK IS PRIMARILY AN ACCOUNT OF A TRIP DOWN THE ALLAGASH River in northern Maine from June 23–25, 2000. However, several other wilderness canoe trips in Maine are referred to in this work, and it may help the reader to see a list of the significant trips in chronological order.

Moose River—July 31–August 2, 1997
Seboeis River—April 20–21, 1998
Seboeis River (The Return)—May 22–23, 1998
Allagash River—July 1–3, 1999

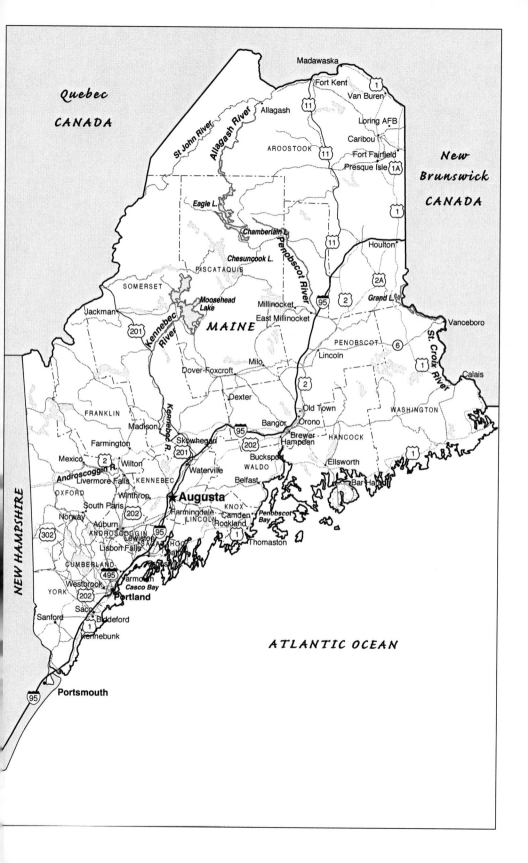

I

IT IS JUNE 14; ONE WEEK BEFORE THE TRIP AND THE DREAD IS SETTING in. My appetite has lessened. I am not enjoying much of anything. I am preoccupied and have trouble being interested in things. A vague but steady nausea floats in my stomach. I feel terribly homesick and haven't even left. I am a psychologist and have been finding talk of my trip intruding into my clients' sessions. This feeling will deepen and broaden in the days to come. I'll watch the weather every chance I get. I will get on the Internet weather sites and look at forecasts for northern Maine. I will be secretly looking for good and honorable reasons to cancel. The dread has been getting worse with each anticipated trip.

The dread was an acquired feeling. I had been raised to ignore and suppress it. You grow up with five brothers in a family like mine and you begin real young to shut it out. A kind of natural selection causes it to weaken in the consciousness and die in the expression. A lifetime of recklessness and good fortune seemed to kill it off altogether. A safe and peaceful adulthood slowly wraps itself around you. Naturally, you come to believe you are safe and that you carry that safety with you. It is a belief deeper than thought, so you don't even notice when you have taken it where it does not belong and it has no power. You develop other mistaken thoughts. People with bad luck think they are cursed. People who've been lucky think they're entitled or that they must be doing something right and that if they've flipped a coin nine times and it's been heads nine times in a row, that it's bound to be heads on the tenth, when in fact the odds are steadily silently growing that it won't.

My friend Kevin is a high school English teacher. Three years ago I told him of a canoe trip I planned to take, alone, in April, down the remote Seboeis River in north central Maine. I had been very excited. I had planned it for months. All winter long I had thought of it in a hundred versions, contingencies and conditions. Every night I brought it to sleep with me like some dream of pirates' treasure. Many nights I got out of bed to write down an idea on how to cope with a newly imagined and adventurous danger, a new piece of equipment, a better way to pack or stow my gear. I had planned to go in late April, during the school vacation, because the ice would be gone, because the flies would not have risen and because I just couldn't wait. Kevin is an ex-Marine, a former football and hockey player. He's been a fisherman and a sailor. He, his wife, and another couple sailed to Australia a few years back. He's a big and burly white-haired, white-bearded pug, who doesn't scare easily. You could say that he is a tough guy and a brave one too. But what I had in mind bothered him and one day he told his class about it, adding that I was an "idiot" for doing this sort of thing alone and that he was angry at me for taking that kind of risk. At the time it made me smile. I was proud to have Kevin view me as so audacious (though he hadn't said "audacious," he'd said "idiot"), skimming right past the fact that he thought me a fool.

There is a lot to be afraid of on a solo wilderness canoe trip. But I had to learn that, piece by piece. For instance, I had believed that I was not afraid of bears. Ignorance and the influence of deep-seated childhood images barred me from the truth. As a child I'd had a full Davy Crockett outfit: a leather fringed jacket, powder horn, canteen, flintlock and coonskin hat. Davy and I not only had the same first name, I often pointed out, but the same initials, D.C. Davy could just "grin" a bear into cuddly submission. I'd seen him do it plenty of times on Walt Disney. That was pretty much the level of my thinking as I considered my trip and the possible dangers I might face. Kevin could see that and it made him wince.

2

As for bears, I still like to think that I want to see one. If I see one up close, I expect I'll wish I hadn't. I've read and heard accounts of the power and unpredictability of black bears. I know they can outswim and outrun, outclimb and outfight any human if they feel like it. And now and then they feel like it. A male black bear can weigh 650 pounds, or twice as much as the most fearsome steroid-pumped pro wrestler. While black bears are not in the same class as grizzlies in size, power or aggressivenes, they do occasionally attack and kill humans. This past July a female Canadian biathlete training in Quebec was killed by a black bear. The bear was a nursing sow and it is believed the woman may have come between the bear and her cub. Bears in remote areas with little or no experience with humans are considered most dangerous. Still, only about 40 people are known to have been killed by black bears in North America in the past century, and bear advocates and aficionados are eager to point out that we have a much greater chance of being killed by a bee sting, dog, or lightning than by a bear. But the imaginations of humans, judging from the popularity of state lotteries, are uninhibited by long odds. What about the three teenagers attacked and partially eaten by a single black bear in Ontario in 1978?

One night I camped on a grassy bluff, upriver of Attean Falls, on the Moose River near Jackman, Maine. I had pulled over right before nightfall, just before a heavy rain, lucky to find what was probably the only campable space for a couple of miles in either direction on either bank. I set up and got quickly into my tent without supper, seconds before the rain. A thin muddy animal trail of some sort passed close by my tent through the high damp grass and down the steep slope to the river. I had been excited by its presence. It was my first trip to Maine and I wanted to get as close as possible to anything wild. I woke up the next morning to the sound of something snuffling softly outside very close. I lay still, listening. It may have been only four or five feet away from my tent opening. I badly wanted to know what it was but I thought the sound and movement of unzipping my tent would scare it away before I could see what it was. Also, I discovered, I didn't really want it to know I was there. I was thinking, what if it's a bear?

But the dread is not really about bears. It's not particularly about animals of any kind, though they have made their contributions. A female moose charged me once across shallow water. I had been coasting toward her, camera in hand, on a lonely narrow stretch of that same Moose River in western Maine. It was early evening. I had just passed by the last established campsites I would see for many miles. There would be no others before nightfall. But I had felt too good to stop for the day just yet. I intended to continue another hour or so and find my own spot to camp. I came around a corner and there she was, the first up-close moose I'd ever seen. I felt rewarded for having pushed on past the campsites at Spencer Rips. All I could think of were the pictures and this big old moose being in my frame. It never occurred to me that I was drifting into her house.

As I came abreast of her, no more than fifty feet away, she charged. The water was only a couple of feet deep and with those long legs she could move with ease. Three long crashing splashing steps covered half the distance, then she stopped. I had been staring, but when she came at me I put my head down and paddled as hard as I could. It would have been to no avail had she decided to continue. I kept my eyes averted until I was at a safe distance. It might have helped. My daughter later told me that it was probably a good thing to have done because if moose are anything like horses, they may perceive direct eye contact (I'd been staring and taking pictures, grinning like a madman) as a challenge. A safe thirty yards downstream I looked back. She might have had calves nearby, I thought. I felt simultaneously exhilarated and intimidated. She stared a baleful good riddance.

I don't worry about injury or illness, though I have made myself think carefully about it. I've read books on wilderness first aid. Never having been a Boy Scout, fireman, soldier, or otherwise resourceful person, I am a complete novice to first aid of any kind. So I read with much grimacing and fascination the diagnoses and treatments for shock and the acute stress reaction, hemorrhages and hypothermia, fractures and flail chest. I can't say, though, that I have actually learned anything. One never knows if something's been learned until it can suddenly be recalled later on in an unexpected moment.

But there is value in mental rehearsal so I've imagined myself taking a tumble into rocky rapids and making my way to shore to find that I am injured. How about, let's see, a dislocated shoulder. Yes, that could happen. OK. The book says, if alone, to lie on a flat ledge of some sort and let the injured arm hang straight down. Oh, first tape (duct tape, of course) ten to fifteen pounds of weight to the end of the arm. With fatigue, the arm will relax and the shoulder will slip back into place. Should only take about an hour. Broken lower leg? Apply traction by placing the foot into the cleft of a tree or rock and pull back firmly until the bones have slipped back into place. While proceeding, bite on nearby tree to keep from frightening nearby animals with disturbing screams.

I capsized once going over a low ledge I hadn't bothered to scout and banged my hip on a submerged boulder. I barely felt it at the time, but it raised a baseball-size lump and left me with the nastiest bruise, by far, I've ever had and unable to lie on that side for a month. I know the soft-looking water can be very hard. Still, the possibility of serious injury seems more hypothetical than real to me. I bring lots of medicine. I could get sick, but I never think about it.

Once I thought I might be lost and it was a terrible thing. I lay in my tent that night thinking, how much would I pay just to know where I am? I plan for the possibility. The *Maine Gazetteer* is an excellent series of finely detailed topographical maps, which include most logging roads and trails at a scale of 1:125,000, or 1 inch equals 2 miles. I make two copies of the area I need, laminate them both and keep one in my survival pouch. If I think I need something better I order topos at a scale of 1:24,000 (1 inch equals about $1/3$ mile) from the U.S. Geological Survey. By comparison my AAA Maine road map is 1:679,000, or 1 inch equals 11 miles. As good as the maps are, none of them can tell the real truth about travel across that terrain.

The land that the maps describe looks open, smooth, clean, and neat across a soothing green expanse. Contour lines indicate the prominent changes in elevation, and symbols show the significant wetlands, but nowhere does the map show the mosquitoes and black flies, that bane which Thoreau called "more formidable than wolves." Nor does it show a forest so thick with pine, fir, and spruce of every size that you need your hands and arms as well as your feet and legs to wrestle your way through. It cannot describe the visibility so limited that, without a compass, you'd be lost for sure in the time it takes to say your prayers. You cannot see the fallen trees strewn thickly like pick-up sticks everywhere and every which way at every angle so you can't take three steps in any direction without having to step over, climb over, tightrope down, crouch or crawl beneath some felled giant whose remaining spike-like branches maintain a screen which must be broken through. It cannot fully describe the ground itself; the broken, rock-strewn land, the mini swamps and alder-encased streams with the ever-present boot and clothes soaking damp. For the sun can only weakly reach these dark depths, and near the rivers, ponds, and lakes the morning mist soaks it fresh each day.

Two years ago, on only my second wilderness trip, I was forced to abandon my canoe and walk out of the Seboeis River wilderness region. It took me parts of two days to cover one mile. It was a full body battle nearly every step of the way. The Maine woods, I have learned, are nothing like the forests of home. Thoreau wrote that his woods, the Massachusetts woods, have lost their "wild, damp and shaggy look." I have spent all my life playing in and hiking through the woods of Massachusetts. I have never needed a trail to make my way. Beneath the oaks, white pines, maples, poplars, and birches there is virtually open ground with few serious obstructions. You can almost keep a straight line. It is easy maneuvering around and through the brush, which dots the former pastureland beneath the trees. Most of the north Maine woods has never been pastureland, never smoothed, domesticated, or even inhabited. The forest is ferocious, tenaciously in your face, pressing on you, pushing on you until you want to scream "Back off. Get off of me." But it won't and it is endless.

In the forests of home visibility is good, several hundred feet much of the time. No black flies tunneling into your hair. No dense clouds of mosquitoes that fill your mouth every time you take a breath or crowd onto every exposed inch of flesh.

But there is no sauntering off to see the country, and
10 or 15 rods seems a great way from your companions,

and you come back with the air of a much traveled man, as from a long journey, with adventures to relate, though you may have heard the crackling of the fire all the while,—and at a hundred rods you might be lost past recovery, and have to camp out. It is all mossy and moosey. In some of those dense fir and spruce woods there's hardly room for the smoke to go up. The trees are a standing night, and every fir and spruce which you fell is a plume plucked from night's raven wing.

Henry David Thoreau, *In the Maine Woods*

Bill Bryson wrote of the Maine woods in his account of his journey along the Appalachian Trail, describing them as having a "more ominous, and brooding feel." He continues,

They were unquestionably different from the woods further south—darker, more shadowy, and inclining more to black than green. There were differences in the trees too—more conifers at low levels and many more birches—and scattered through the undergrowth were larger rounded black boulders like sleeping animals, which lent these still recesses a certain eeriness. When Walt Disney made a motion picture of Bambi, his artists based their images on the Great North Woods of Maine, but this was palpably not a Disney forest of roomy glades and cuddlesome creatures. This brought to mind the woods in the Wizard of Oz, where the trees have ugly faces and malign intent and every step seems a gamble. This was a woods for looming bears, dangling snakes, wolves with laser red eyes, strange noises, sudden terrors—a place of "standing night" as Thoreau neatly and nervously put it.

Bill Bryson, *A Walk in the Woods*

I would say that my two-day trek in the Seboeis River area east of Baxter State Park was the worst experience of my life, except that in my winter reveries I find myself thinking back on it wistfully, fantasizing secretly, despite myself, of having to do it again. From the safety of my bed before falling asleep, from the safe distance of the off-season, I pose problems for myself and then try to solve them.

For instance, what if I capsized in fast rapids and became separated from my canoe and all my supplies which had been tied in so securely; my pack, my water, all my gear, everything lost, sent zipping away from me downriver as I crawl to shore?

Following the river along its bank is rarely possible for long. Alders, steep banks, boulders or dense forests to the waterline usually prevent any travel along the river shore. Swamps, the river's twisting path and other impediments will probably wear out any attempt to follow the river from higher ground. If the river is deep enough and not too cluttered with rocks, a raft might be made and poled downstream in search of the lost canoe. I have a book called *How to Stay Alive in the Woods,* by an old-timer named Bradford Angier, which shows how it can be done. I like that idea a lot. But I might just have to set off overland in the direction of the closest logging road marked on my map. In any case I'll have nothing to rely on but what I'm wearing, the contents of my fisherman's vest and my waist survival pouch. The contents of the survival pouch fall roughly into five categories: warmth, shelter, water, physical care and travel. "Dry" comes under the headings of warmth and shelter.

To stay warm and dry I have, first of all, lots of matches. In a waterproof, screw-top, rubber-gasketed little tube I have wooden friction matches. The plastic tube is in a waterproof plastic box. It's a small one, about the size of my hand. I've checked it, though, weighted down in a sink full of water, and found it leaks a bit. The tube doesn't. In a plastic bag, the "one-zip" Hefty brand—the best because it has that little white sliding clasp that seals up easily even in the dark or with shaky hands—I keep waterproof and regular matches. These are stuffed into the box as well. Both types have their limitations. The waterproof ones have tiny sulfur heads that break off and don't light that easily, and if their strike plate gets wet they won't light at all. Regular paper matches light great but of course are useless wet. I figure that with the three types I can get a fire lit. Just in case there are no birch trees around, I carry bark in the pouch. The final item in the waterproof box is a tiny flashlight into which I must remember to put a fresh AA battery.

The hatchet on my belt can help prepare firewood (or make that raft) and help in building a shelter. All that is needed is readily available. Trees give you the material for a lean-to. I pack a 4 X 8-foot piece of heavy plastic for a waterproof roof that can be covered with the branches of whatever evergreen is most lush and most available. I keep a small roll of nylon string for tying things down and together, though I've read that arborvitae or hemlock bark in strips makes excellent string. With a fire and a shelter you can start getting dry and warm if you are wet and cold. I pack a space blanket to wrap around myself as well. It folds up to the size of a hot dog bun, weighs nothing and will wrap around your body, preserving any heat your body can produce, or so I hear; I've never had to use one. A small bottle of insect spray is included so that I'm not sucked dry as a raisin while sitting in my lean-to. There are reliable accounts of deer and moose being killed by blood loss due to the mosquitoes and flies. Humans are simply driven mad. I wonder what the Indians did for protection? The Indian guide with Thoreau used nothing and suffered for it.

> The Indian would not use our wash to protect his face and hands, for fear that it would hurt his skin, nor had he any veil; he, therefore, suffered from insects now, and throughout this journey, more than either of us I think.
>
> Thoreau, *In the Maine Woods*

The survival pouch is where I keep my water purification tablets. I have my canteen on my belt and a light plastic water container folded up in my pouch. Even apparently pristine wilderness streams cannot be entirely trusted to be free of diarrhea-causing microbes.

In case I get hurt I include a small first-aid kit with bandages, gauze, antiseptic ointment, medicine in a waterproof plastic screw-top container, an Ace bandage and a nylon knee brace for my vulnerable, football-loosened knees.

I have a Leatherman combination knife, a type of Swiss Army knife containing a toolbox full of devices you could build a schooner with and still have puzzling instruments left unused. I have yet to have a need for it, but it's small and was a Christmas gift and comes in a nice leather holder and in an emergency might have just the thing I need, buried somewhere in its midst.

The pouch is where I keep my car keys, cash, and credit cards, all thoroughly bagged. After all, presuming I make my way to civilization or to wherever it is my truck has been left for me, I'll need these things. If my truck has been, instead, merrily appropriated by impoverished unscrupulous shuttlers who considered my rusted, dented, never-been-to-a-car wash-or-in-any-other-way-properly-washed, handmade-by-my-hands-wooden-canoe-rack-bearing, 1990 Ford F-150 (with air-conditioning and power locks and windows) two-wheel-drive (what was I thinking?) beast to be such a major improvement over their own vehicles that they just couldn't help themselves and were willing to throw away their reputations as honorable shuttlers in order to have it, then I'll really need the money and credit cards.

I have my compass and laminated map. Now if I truly *were* to find myself without or unable to use my canoe, the safe and smart thing would be to stay by the river and wait for someone to eventually come by. Even in the wilderness, rivers are roads and people travel them a lot more than they travel deep uninhabited trackless forests. In addition you will be where you told your family you would be, along the river, so searchers will know where to look if you're late returning home. But it could be that the waiting is unendurable or undesirable for some reason or that the wait could amount to days and a dirt road leading to a ranger station or a frequently used canoe put-in point may pass nearby, with a vehicle now and then passing along it. Some logging roads see a good deal of use. On the other hand there are usually more trails and old roads in the woods than are marked on the maps, and getting lost in the maze they can create is a very real danger. It's usually best to stay put.

Finally and least important according to all the guidebooks is food. Nonetheless, I will be sure to enclose a few energy bars of some sort this time. Though it is said that a person can go many days without food they rarely wish to, and so I will include some food because one can only be so content living on mouthfuls of mosquitoes.

I will be wearing a hat and prescription sunglasses, if I haven't lost them. For the first time, on the upcoming trip, I will have a pair in reserve in my survival pouch. I will probably have a nylon quick-drying T-shirt, Gore-Tex shorts and a pair of sneakers. I will have a skin diver's knife ($3^1/2$-inch blade) strapped to my calf. I love my knife. I've never owned a gun or any sort of weapon in my life. While it's a very useful tool, I know I wear it mainly because it looks so cool. On my belt I will have a one-liter canteen along with the hatchet. While I have packed and repacked the contents of the waist pouch many times, I have never had to open it on a trip. I have imagined the use of each of its precious items in great detail.

The greatest danger to any person in a wilderness survival situation is cold. Cold scares me. Hypothermia can break down or kill a person faster than anything short of traumatic injury or poisoning. Much faster than heat, thirst, or hunger. It is my greatest fear. It is one source of the dread. Whenever I imagine myself in a miserable wilderness condition I see myself cold and wet. Cold and wet is just what I would be if I lost my canoe and had to walk out. Even in summer the water in Maine can be cold, the woods damp and shady, the nights very cool. Cold water dissipates heat faster than any other commonly encountered substance, faster than wind, 240 times faster than still air.

I had a taste of the early stages of hypothermia a couple of years ago. I had returned with a friend to the Seboeis River in late May to retrieve the canoe I had been forced to abandon there the month before. That ill-advised (idiotic) April trip had culminated in the horrific two-day hike out.

It was a bit warmer in May, but not much. The snow was gone from the woods. The river level had dropped considerably from its April flood stage. It was drizzly, barely in the 50s. The forest was filled with mist and the low clouds seemed to grow up out of it. Everything, the water, the sky, the trees, was washed in shades of gray and black. Dismal.

Paul is my age. We met on our high-school football team and have been friends ever since. He has only slightly more woodsman experience than I, but he's strong, tough, and about as indefatigable as a person can be. He has slowed his exuberant recklessness a little, over time, but still sneers at danger and enjoys what we used to call "good torture," which loosely translated means something like "pleasure in hardship in the service of a good cause and/or good story." A good cause is nearly anything that yields a good story.

The retrieval of the canoe seemed to offer excellent opportunities for "good torture." Though we hadn't spoken for several months he had agreed in an instant to accompany me. Agreement, for Paul, did not automatically evolve into preparation, though when I picked him up at 4:00 A.M. and he threw his hockey duffel bag into the back of my truck, he looked well supplied to me. So I was surprised when, just past Bangor, he told me to get off at the next exit. "I have to get a couple of things." We found a Wal-Mart and we rushed in and picked up a box of plastic trash bags. "These will be my raincoat if I need it." Outside it was raining lightly. "Probably rig up a bunch of them for my tent, too." He wanted some hiking boots but didn't like their prices.

"Jeez, Paul, do you need anything else? No *tent*? I told you I only had a one-man tent? What *did* you bring?"

"Oh I'm fine. Don't worry about it. I got everything. Hmm, mosquito repellent. I could use that."

It is a shame to go to the Maine woods and not see a moose. I nearly hit two on a desolate road as it neared the river. Paul had just said to me, "You know, you should probably slow down some. There could be moose in the road anywhere." I looked at him to see if he was joking. Caution and foresight had never been particular qualities of his. But he was right. So I slowed down and there they were around the next curve, a cow and her calf. They quickly glanced at us, then loped into the woods without a sound, snaked between the trees, and were gone. Seeing them and missing them seemed to be good omens. Unfortunately the incident also encouraged Paul's belief that he is psychic.

I had left my canoe on the west bank, pulled up ten feet from the high waterline. Our task was to hike down a trail along the east side a mile or so and locate the canoe on the opposite side. Unbeknownst to me a month ago, there was an abandoned old logging road running parallel to the river about a quarter mile above the water on the west side.

We spotted the canoe, now a good 30 feet from the water, took the truck down the bumpy dirt track, branches scraping roughly along both sides, to its end, which was at a point below which we estimated the canoe would lie.

Blankets of mosquitoes draped themselves over us the moment we left the truck. I counted eight of them on just one of Paul's fingers. What do they do all day without people to suck on? Torment the deer and moose, I guess.

He laughed, "Good thing I got this stuff, huh?" as we quickly doused ourselves with the DEET.

The woods presented a solid mass into which we plunged hands first like tunnelers. I put my head nearly into Paul's back and followed him in. How hard could it be? Go straight. Head downhill as soon as the ground began to slope to the river. Our ears alone should be able to guide us. Within five minutes or fifty yards we'd each fallen down at least once and the forest had turned us in so many directions we no longer had any idea which way was north, south, east, or west or where to point for the river or the road. It hadn't seemed necessary to take a compass reading to walk 400 yards to a river. But, this being the Maine woods, we were immediately engulfed and disoriented. The compass set us right and following it carefully we soon made out flickers of the white-capped lead gray river between the trees. A few minutes more and there was the canoe right in front of us, exactly as I had left it in the snowy woods of April a month before.

II

THE SEBOEIS RIVER IN APRIL HAD BEEN A SWOLLEN ROILING RUSH OF ice-cold Class III and IV rapids, a fearsome mixture of standing three-foot waves, splashing, twisting currents and boulder-strewn obstacle courses. This is what happens when a lot of water gets pinched into a narrow space and hurried by gravity downhill as fast as it can go. It was far more than I had expected or had the skills for. I had failed to recall the notation in bold print in the Appalachian Mountain Club's *Maine River Guide* warning that rapid ratings must be raised as much as one or two levels at very high water. The Class II rapids I had expected had been amplified by the heavy spring flow. But I had waited eight months and driven seven hours in a spattering rain and was not about to turn back.

The put-in spot was in a campsite just above the Grand Lake Road bridge, one of the few paved roads in the area. In late spring and summer the spot would be lined with large family-size tents and campers bustling with smoky cookouts and talk of fishing. It was a lonely and forlorn place in April. In Massachusetts it was early spring. In this part of Maine it was still the end of winter. On the drive in I'd noticed lakes and ponds still half frozen and patches of white in the woods. Worry grew within me, but the business of driving the winding road and the search for the put-in held my full attention. I had to get out of the truck to change.

The rain drifted down in a soft mist. I took off all my clothes except my shorts and T-shirt in order to pull on the wet suit. My hands were shaking. It was cold, but not that cold. Everything felt uncomfortable, the tight stiff wet suit, the ominous weather and me. I pulled my canoe to the landing and loaded up. I worked as quickly as I could. My hands fumbled with the ropes, strings, buckles, and straps. Activity focused my thoughts but a grim uneasiness throbbed within me. The swollen river stuffed itself noisily under the bridge. I would be going very fast from the moment I got in. Yet it was as if my mind had shut off. As I prepared to shove off I took no last look around, no moment for conscious speculation or anticipation, no final check or final words. I just got in, turned my bow into the flow and went under the bridge. The river weaves its way due south with no sharp angles or turns. Most of its rocks and boulders were submerged beneath the flood. But it pulled me crashing through row after row of high standing waves that bounced me around so hard I could hardly keep my paddle in the water. Water was splashing on me from over the bow. Some was getting in over the sides. I was unnerved and couldn't plan ahead. All I could think was, don't let it turn me sideways.

Almost immediately I was wide-eyed and struggling for control. A mile and a half from the put-in was Grand Pitch, a seventy-five-yard series of steep rocky drops channeled between high cliffs, unnavigable by any sort of craft and probable death in a canoe, and I was heading there fast. I forgot all about the only portage trail around the falls being on the left. I only knew I had to get out before I capsized and was swept over. I headed for the nearest bank, which happened to be the right or west bank, paddling with all my might while making sure I didn't turn myself broadside to the torrent. When I got close enough I reached for protruding alder branches and pulled myself to land.

I stood on the shore, ten minutes into my trip, stunned and wretched with the realization that I could go no further, while a freezing drizzle formed a light crust on the shoulders of my wet suit.

A little scouting assured me that there was no way I could portage around the falls on this side of the river. Swamps, cliffs, deep snow, and impenetrable forest cleared away any possibility of carrying a sixteen-foot, sixty-five-pound canoe more than a few yards. I certainly could not

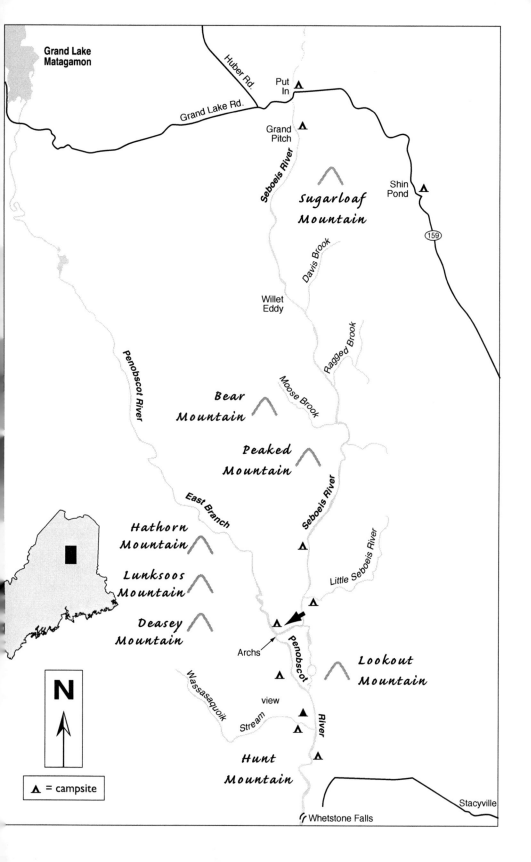

cross the river to the other side. I would have to leave the canoe and walk out. I clipped two canteens to my belt and left the rest of my water behind. At the time I didn't know about the old logging road. I hoisted my fifty-pound pack onto my back and headed off through the snow into the woods guided by the simple intention of keeping in sight of the river, knowing I would eventually reach the road and my truck. It didn't take a whole lot of thought. My focus was short and tight, no deeper or broader than the places to plant my feet and hands or the method to get past the fallen trees always blocking my path. The previous winter had laid the worst ice storm in 100 years on Maine and knocked over all but its strongest trees, leaving the forest floor a vast landscape of wreckage.

The wet suit was the perfect body armor in this place. It protected me from the damp that slid down every trunk and branch and hung from every leaf and needle. It shielded me from the branches, which scratched and tore. It was a rental. When I sheepishly returned it a week later I seriously doubted they would accept it. It looked like it had been raked by machine-gun fire.

The pack was far too heavy for this terrain. I was constantly thrown off balance by its weight as I clambered over wet rocks and trees. Little of what I did could be called walking. It was climbing, crawling, teetering, falling. Slowing down helped a bit. I had been needlessly hurrying. Still, I continued to fall down, risking a wide variety of leg injuries. I didn't think about it at the time, but any one of them could have hobbled me or worse, resulting in the most dire of consequences.

I was unaware of the time until the thick cloud cover began to bring an early end to the day. I had yet to pass any patch of ground suitable for even my small tent. Then I came upon a swamp. It was deeper and wider than I wished to cross so I broke my rule and left the river, going deeper into the woods looking for a way around. I soon found one and turned back in what I took to be a straight line to the water. From the time I had left the canoe I had kept the river firmly on my right shoulder heading north, upstream. But as I rounded the swamp and tried to return to my course, moving water appeared on my left. I was too exhausted at that moment to consider the implications of this. I dropped my pack on the spot in the first clearing I had seen in four hours of travel, dumped myself heavily against a tree and unzipped the neck of my suit. My chest was heaving and I was soaked in sweat. Thick steam rose warmly around my face. Reaching for my belt, I found that I had lost one of my canteens.

After a drink I began to think about the water rushing past nearby. How could it be on my left? Is it a swollen converging stream? I could remember none marked on my map in this area. Then again, I couldn't recall a swamp being marked either. I was worried. I went to my pack for my map and compass. I wore no waist pouch back then. I searched the top pockets and then the rear, and then the sides. I opened the pack up. They weren't there. I was confused. Then it struck me. I must have left them in the boat. I would have to go back.

I couldn't accept this at first and bravely whimpered, "oh no, oh no, oh no," probably on the verge of tears, until I steadied myself. Having no choice helps one focus. I pitched my tent, laid out my sleeping bag, took a long drink of water and looked for my trail back to the canoe. Without the pack it was much easier and safer going and I made good time. Though it became dark the snow held some light and the prints of my footsteps easily guided my way. That which had been a hindrance had become a help.

I found the canoe and in the bottom lay my vest holding my laminated map, compass, insect spray, and suntan lotion. I have no idea why I had taken it off. I retraced my steps once more, plodding slowly, head down, searching for the trail in the forest dark. The sweat inside my wet suit had cooled and I began to feel the chill of the night. I crawled into my tent in the pitch black wearing warm dry clothes and got into my bag. I hadn't eaten since 9:00 that morning but felt no hunger, only some thirst and the nagging question, where am I?

I got out my flashlight and studied the map. It showed no stream. Could it be a tiny unmarked brook flooded to significance by the spring melt? If so, it was blocking my way and would be difficult and dangerous if not impossible to cross. But my compass showed that it flowed north to south just like the river. Perhaps it *was* the river. It made all the sense in the world that it would be. Yet, I could not orient myself to it and could not shake that fearful question, how did it end up on the other side of me?

I lay in my tent that night thinking of many things. How cold would it get and would my 40-degree sleeping bag and all my clothes be enough to keep me warm? I could not risk injury spending the next day carrying that full pack. What should I leave behind to lighten my load? It would, in part, depend on whether I could finish before nightfall the next day. But what if I was lost? If it was a stream splashing outside my tent, how would I cross it? What could I take across with me? I thought about how much I'd pay just to know where I was.

I lay with my eyes wide open in the deep black, struck by the pitilessness of the wilderness, realizing that Nature cares nothing for the individual. The individual tree. The individual fish. The individual fly. Only the whole. Only the system. And *that* it maintains relentlessly, dispassionately. The individual means nothing. In *Heart of Darkness,* of his river journey, Conrad wrote of Nature as malevolent: "and this stillness of life did not in the least resemble a peace. It was the stillness of an implacable force brooding over an inscrutable intention. It looked at you with a vengeful aspect."

I didn't feel that way. I felt instead that Nature took no notice of me at all. That I could die beneath its gaze, lie down and decompose and never be noticed. Nature is not my friend or enemy. It is far above and beyond that. It is too great to care. It gave me a very lonely feeling.

The civilization in which I live is an environment cluttered with elements for the care of Man. It is thinking of the care of Man all the time. If I look out the window of the house I live in, that temple to the care of man, I see a paved road. It is more than wide enough for two cars. Two trucks even. It is well made. Domed slightly so that water will run off to the sides. It has freshly painted lines. White on the outside so the driver at night can see where the road ends and the non-road begins. Special reflective paint was used. Two bright unbroken yellow lines run down the middle warning drivers that it is unsafe to pass. Just down the road a bit there are strong steel guardrails planted on either side. They have been placed there in particular because behind them the land drops off steeply. So they wait there for as long as it takes, standing guard to hold in any vehicle, any sleepy driver who may veer beyond the bright white line, to care for him. Across the street from my house a road enters perpendicularly. A stop sign informs the driver he should stop, wait, and look, so he may safely proceed. Up the road a yellow sign bearing a **T** lying on its side warns drivers about the road that enters perpendicularly. There are street signs so you won't get lost. There are telephone poles bearing electric power lines. Today a big truck came with one of those buckets that hoists a man way up into the air. They'd come to cut tree limbs away from power lines. They went 70 feet up with a chain saw to cut a whole lot of branches off of my tree. Branches which any heavy snow or ice storm might have weighed down, snapping those power lines. We have created a world that takes care of us so well that when it is stripped away leaving us nothing but Nature, we're left cringing and confused and imagine that Nature is against us. It isn't against us. It simply isn't *for* us.

I lay there knowing I was on my own. But wasn't that what I had come for and why I had come alone? I stayed warm by putting on every bit of clothing I had. I kept wondering if it would be enough. I slept little, but enough to be startled by the sun glowing through my tent. I got out into a crisp clear dawn. It was cold. Ice covered the top of my tent and crackled with the movement of the fabric. My boots were frozen and my wet suit stood stiff like a suit of armor against the tree where it hung. But the world was full of color. No more gray. Instead a brilliant blue sky, sparkling blue water, a dozen shades of rich shiny green and the gleaming white of the snow and birch. It was a beautiful morning.

I put on my warmest socks, stuck them into a double layer of plastic bags and shoved them into my ice-hard boots. There was a sunny spot that was free of snow. The ground there was covered by a delicate green matting of moss sprinkled with brown pine needles. I prepared a fire with dead branches broken off the lower levels of the trees and started it with bark curling off a nearby birch. I felt good and a little like a real woodsman. I heated a can of nice, hot soup and felt comfortable and fortified. Across the water a fox emerged from the bushes. It held something dead in its mouth. It eyed me for a moment then slipped back into the forest. I sat on the softness with my back against a tree. The sun was warm on my chest. I think I was smiling.

I packed. I left behind half my canned food (I'd packed enough for a three-day canoe camping trip), my wet suit, and my tent. I kept my sleeping bag, all my clothes and my cooking gear. I set off lightly. Everything was easier. The snow had taken on a firm crust of ice, courtesy of yesterday's rain and the freezing night. It let me walk on it rather than sink into it with every other step as on the day before. The woods became clearer and there were few blowdowns. I came across the tracks of a moose and followed them, believing it would pick the best way, and it did. In two hours I had reached the road and my truck. I emptied my pack and went back for the rest of my stuff, enjoying the walk. In the clear light of day it was fairly easy to comprehend what had baffled me the day before. Apparently the water, which had appeared on my left and freaked me out, had been the river all along. When I had curled around the swamp I'd curled too far, bringing me around it into a near circle as I returned to the river.

I'd had some serious difficulties on my first wilderness trip to Moose River the summer before. Arriving home battered and bitterly humbled, I announced to my family ("Uh, Dad where's your canoe?"), "That's it. Maine hates me. I'm not going outside anymore. Not even going to look out the window."

III

AND NOW I WAS BACK, A MONTH LATER WITH PAUL. AND AGAIN IT WAS raining.

Here are our whiney excuses for what happened next. My cheap no-good canoe, it turned out, carried only 660 pounds, or so said the metal information disc riveted to the bow. I'll bet the truth was more like 560. Paul and I weigh between 180 and 200 pounds each. Include our gear and the case of beer Paul insisted on getting despite my telling him I didn't want any, to which he replied, "Oh sure, and then when I start drinking you'll want some and drink all mine." Finally, add the weight of all the water, which soon saturated us and our stuff and sloshed around in the bottom of our boat, and we quickly became overloaded.

Next, the canoe carries a depth at the center thwart of less than thirteen inches. Fully loaded and not counting the weight of the water we soon took on, the gunwales were only about three inches above the splashing waterline—not nearly enough in any kind of rapids. Certainly not with us at the controls. It has a keel. This is of no use in rapids. It makes quick turning nearly impossible and interferes terribly with the frequent necessity of sliding over rocks and ledges. You tend to get hung up, then suddenly tip on the keel, sending you into a jerking attempt at stabilization, which is as likely to tip you all the way over as to balance you out. Finally, we didn't know what the hell we were doing. Minimal experience and no coordination between us proved to be nasty ingredients under the circumstances. We capsized three or four times in a quarter mile, maybe more. They began to blend together after a while. That was it. We pulled over to the east bank portage, carried around the falls, and at 2:30 P.M. called it quits for the day.

A half a mile. Not bad. Only twenty-two miles to go to reach the end of the trip and my truck which I had arranged to have shuttled down there by a scar-faced, bleary-eyed wreck of a guy who you would cross the street to avoid if he came near you in your town. But I gave him $60 and the keys to my truck because, out there, you can't pick and choose.

My gear was pretty dry. I had bagged my clothes before putting them in my pack. But my book was wet and so was the edge of my sleeping bag, which for some reason I had forgotten to double bag. My food was fine, all canned. My matches were waterproof and securely bagged. Paul hadn't bagged anything, leaving him with no dry clothes and a wet sleeping bag to go along with his no tent. Sadly he had also liquefied the hot dog rolls and cheese curls he'd been so proud to contribute. Only his beer was unaffected.

We set up the tarp as a shelter from the persistent rain and set about getting wood for a fire. We had no hatchet or saw. But Paul cheerfully went about slaughtering and dismembering standing deadwood until we had a fine pile of semi-dry firewood, which lit easily.

It warmed us, but we could find no way to get our stuff dry. The air was saturated with moisture. The falls gave off a constant cloud of suspended vapor, which filled the forest all about. Everything around us, every rock, stump, and tree, every surface alive or dead, every inch of untrodden ground was covered with a bright green moss. It was quite beautiful, like woodlands I've seen in Ireland or the rainforests of the Pacific Northwest. Add to this the rain and we had no climate for drying. It seemed that as fast as moisture would steam away from our shoes, clothes, and sleeping bags, the liquid air would replace it.

We were glad to see the day end. I got into my tent. Paul crawled under the canoe. We both slept badly. The damp made it hard to really feel warm. I listened to the rain all night.

We got up early to a drizzly dawn and the same dreary gray sun that had weakly shone through the same thick clouds the day before. I love the early morning along a river in the woods, but on that morning I did not want to come out of my tent.

We wrung out everything that was wet as best we could, not to make it dry, since that was impossible, but to lessen its weight. We poured out the remaining beer. There seemed no point in putting on dry clothes just to get them wet and we had little reason to feel confident that this day we could perform any better than the day before. Our remaining dry clothes had to be conserved, that is, my remaining dry clothes. Paul had no remaining dry clothes. So we put our cold wet clothes back on, took a deep breath and headed back into the river and the rapids. At least we would have a full day to deal with it. But our spirits were pretty good, not exactly happy but at least able to muster up some grim humor. We had "good torture" by the bucketful.

Paul sat in the back and could see right away that we were riding higher in the water. That gave us a lift. We handled the initial set of Class II+ rapids and big waves fine, steering smoothly around some well-spaced boulders. Our confidence grew. Our communication and coordination of strokes got better and we started to relax. Then it became fun.

We were flying down the river. It was filled with treacherous rocks. We let the water do a lot of the work for us, taking us by better paths than we might have chosen. We stopped fighting it. Relaxation was the key. We rode it the way you should ride a horse. Once we lapsed and crashed head-on into a large rock, but the boat just bounced straight back and the water smoothly took us around it. Soon the flow slowed to moderate current and we settled into a regular paddling pace. We had set off at 6:00 A.M. At a pace of three to four miles an hour we expected to reach the logging road bridge at Whetstone Falls by around noon. We very much hoped the truck would be waiting.

The air remained wet and cool, probably in the low 40s only to rise to the mid-50s. We began wet and didn't get any drier. Paul's legs and hands were cold. His cotton jeans held chilly water close against his skin. I had on light 100 percent nylon L. L. Bean "paddling pants" which held very little water. Besides cold feet, I felt pretty good. Most important, my chest and upper body were warm. My hands are nearly always warm, even on cold winter days. I rarely need gloves, but I had some with me to guard against blisters and gave them to Paul.

By 9:00 A.M. he was having trouble. Years of sports, including several years in college and professional hockey, had left their mark. His back was beginning to hurt him and for him to even mention it, it had to be bad. He tried standing. I didn't like that at all. We were cold and heavy enough as we were; another drenching would not be a good thing. It didn't help him anyway. Nothing did. I told him to just lie back and I'd paddle all the way. But he couldn't get comfortable. It only got worse. We decided to pull over somewhere and see if walking around a bit would do any good. There are no prepared campsites along this stretch of the river. None marked on my map for the rest of the trip. Natural clearings are virtually nonexistent along Maine wilderness rivers. The dense forest hugs the shore tightly, leaning over the river which tunnels its way through. Finding a place to get out and walk around on semi-level ground would not be easy. After a very long and, for Paul, agonizing hour, we found one. A logging road terminated at the river in a broad flat dirt cul-de-sac. A perfect spot.

We pulled up beneath the steep ten-foot high riverbank. Paul got out stiffly. I caught my foot on something and fell out, landing sideways in two feet of water and completely soaked myself. Paul laughed. I was mortified. I had felt so lucky to be free of pain and cold. But I found no fault in Paul's reaction. I'd have done the same to him.

When we reached the top of the bank and the exposed clearing the wind hit us. Sitting low in the river, beneath the trees and the high banks, we had been protected from it, hadn't even known there was a breeze in the air. Before I had taken ten steps I was shivering so hard I couldn't speak. My jaw was bouncing up and down like a terrified cartoon character's. It was a cold unlike any I had ever felt, completely unlike the frigid cold of winter that comes from outside you and stings the surface of your skin. This cold came from inside, as if it emanated from my core. It was a thought-stopping sensation. I could no longer remember what I was doing there. Paul was more clearheaded. "We have to make a fire. Come on." He led me into the woods for firewood and to get out of the wind. It was only with stern concentration that I was able to direct my actions. I felt slow and weak and labored in my thinking. Paul, despite his back problems, moved with a lot more energy and focus than I, but he could not handle the matches. When he tried he found his hands shaking as my jaw and body had been, and could not do it. So I tried, again aided by the birch bark that I always carry with me, which will light as well wet or dry. I bore down with the intensity of a diamond cutter, willing my hands to stay steady. Later I recalled the old *Saturday Night Live* skit where the bearded rabbi performs a circumcision while riding in the back seat of a car, a mock commercial for the smooth ride of the new model Cadillac. Like the rabbi, I succeeded and we soon had a large and smoky fire going. Soon our shivering stopped. But the moment we walked away from the fire, as I did to get a dry shirt from my pack in the canoe, the cold wind hit hard again, penetrating our clothing and chilling us immediately. I know now that we should have eaten a larger breakfast and/or a hearty hot meal as we stood around our fire, that food is a fuel that warms one's insides like an internal heat-producing engine. But the thought never entered our minds. We thought that only the exercise of paddling in the low protected river valley would give us any lasting warmth, as it had earlier. The walking had done Paul's back some good and he discovered that kneeling was by far his best position. In that way we made it without further incident to the bridge, the truck, and the giddy warmth of the full-blasting heater.

So I know a little of hypothermia, the edge of it anyway. But I also know what I don't know and I don't know anything about real hardship; nothing about what real explorers on real expeditions have felt. My worst day would have been Shackleton's best.

My father was with the First Marine Division at Guadalcanal, so he's done some extended camping. He knew about it. But he only told the funny stories. My older brother Tom was in Vietnam. Like most combat soldiers (101st Airborne) he doesn't tell many stories. He had been home from Vietnam for a few weeks when our mother came out of his bedroom with a startled look on her face and two flat rectangular boxes in her hands. We were eating at the oversized trestle table in our kitchen that sat six boys, a girl, and a mother and father.

"What are these?" she said to Tom. Her tone was weird. Anxious, worried, and somehow accusing. Total silence. No one got in Tom's face. Even my mother was careful with him. His temper was volcanic and had gained him a good deal of fame and trouble on the nighttime streets of our city before he went to war. I leaned forward and looked down the row of brothers to what she held but couldn't make it out. What could it be and what would he do? My mother stuck the boxes between his plate and his nose.

"I found these in your drawer."

Jesus, what were they? Drugs? Stolen goods? What? He was slow to react to her, but when she shoved the boxes under his face and he took a look, he slammed down his fork and knife and everything jumped— plates, glasses, us. I could see his face had burst out in red and his jaw muscles quivered along the side of his face. He snatched the boxes out of her hands, stood up, gave her a death stare and went to his room. He slammed the door behind him and did not come out.

My father wasn't afraid of Tom or anyone else and I didn't think he'd stand for this, but it happened so fast he didn't have time to react. We all sat there, mouths and forks suspended in motion, looking at my mother, my father, and Tom's empty space.

"I was putting some things away in his drawer and found those things at the bottom, under his underwear," she said. "Medals. Bronze Stars with citations. He never told me anything about that," she said, stunned, offended, and now embarrassed. It was fifteen years until my brother Donny and I got him to tell us the stories behind those boxes, the only time he has before or since.

Now, if I ask him very specific questions, he'll talk about certain aspects of life in the war and seems to enjoy it a bit. But I have to ask the right question and when I do it's like his brain goes click and his eyes light up and out rolls a story. I had asked him something about sleeping in the jungle. He told about a time he and his platoon were slipping and sliding up and down very steep terrain in the central high- lands. All sharp angles with no flat ground anywhere. In conditions like that, and they were not rare, they would simply tie themselves to a tree and doze sitting up.

"I remember one night sitting in the pouring rain. It had been raining for days. I was just sitting in my poncho staring out from under my hood and thinking, this is awful. This is just awful." He said it real slow. Awful. It's one of those words that sounds like what it means. When I hear that word now, I think of how he used it and try to remember to give myself a good slap when I get a little wet, or cold, or tired and make the mistake of thinking I'm miserable, because I don't know what awful is. I've heard some people my age say there is a kind of guilt that floats around in the guys of my generation who never fought a war like our fathers and brothers did. As if we've missed out on something or maybe our lives have gotten too safe and easy and we're looking for a little hardship and that's why the survival/adventure books and trips are so popular now. As if those experiences could make up for what we missed and others have endured. As for my brother, he looks at my photos, smiling with some interest but shakes his head and says, "I've had enough camping."

It was nice being with Paul on that trip back to the Seboeis and I'll do it again. But despite the near foolishness of it, I prefer to go alone. I always feel that I come up short in saying why. I know that I like the simplicity of it. Planning alone is at least twice as easy as planning with another. I know that my focus on the experience is much better, more pure. I am not distracted by conversation or the expectation of conversation. I'm not wondering if my partner is tired or if my own pace is sufficient or if he wants a meal or to camp or where to camp or when to start or when to stop or whether to come in out of the wind or rain. Instead there is only me to think of these things, me with the experience of it, with nothing in between. And it's the tight focus on the experience that I go for and from which the best memories come.

IV

My plan for the upcoming June trip is to drive five and a half hours to Millinocket, Maine, to Jim Stang's place. He runs, well he *is*, Katahdin Air Service off of a long T-dock in Spencer Cove, a part of Ambajejus Lake in central Maine. There my canoe will be tied to the pontoon of one of his little single-engine floatplanes. My gear will be stowed and we'll climb into the two tiny front seats for the $180 ride between the mountains, past the granite bulk of Mount Katahdin and into the Allagash River region of northern Maine. It will be about a one-hour flight tightly encased in the hot, loud, brain rattling cockpit of a light windblown plane. Nauseating, to anyone with a vulnerability to motion sickness like me, but well worth the time it saves; a one hour flight rather than an additional four hours of driving on axle-jarring dirt roads. I say that now because the memory of how sick I felt last time has faded. I can barely remember having thought to myself, put me down anywhere. There would be fine, right in that huge lake. I don't hate lakes anymore. It'd be great. Right there. My truck will be delivered, by people unknown to me but whom Jim will hire for about $125, to the yard of an elderly widow in Allagash Village, where the Allagash meets the St. John along the Quebec border at that little cleft at the most northern tip of Maine.

Evelyn McBraierty lives alone, a short walk up from the gravelly landing, and stores vehicles for a dollar a day. Last July, due to some weird circumstances I'll go into later, I finished an Allagash trip at 5:30 A.M., way too early to be waking this lady up to get my truck. So I took my time emptying my canoe, washing my face and changing my clothes. About 6:00 A.M. I walked up to see where the house was. It was easy to find, being close by and the only one in the area, a nice old two-story white farmhouse with a big front porch. Three pickup trucks, mine included, were parked in her green well-kept side lawn. I thought I'd check it out and started up the long driveway when the screen door opened and out she came onto her porch as if I were a tardy dinner guest and she'd been watching for me through her window.

"Lo theya. Lookin' for a veehicle?" she called strongly down to me, still a hundred feet away.

"I didn't want to wake you up. I didn't think anybody'd be up yet."

"Oh, I'm up alright. Don't sleep much," she smiled. She had thick white-gray hair and wore a faded flowered housedress. She was fairly tall with broad shoulders and a straight back. She had me come inside without the slightest uncertainty or hesitation. Glad to have the company I guess. Just inside the door was a large kitchen and there on her round old aluminum and Formica table were sets of keys, labeled with torn scraps of white paper in the broad gray strokes of a dull pencil.

"That'll be four dollars. A dollar a day for the truck and a dollar for the canoe. My daddy ran the last ferry 'cross the river [Allagash] 'fore they put the wood bridge up. He charged one dollar each way. So that's what I ask, one dollar."

Our business was done but I felt gently held by her. She picked up a white booklet from the table and opened it. It was more a thick pamphlet than a book and seemed filled with grainy black and white photos and double-spaced print. She told me the name of the village woman who had written it and continued looking into its pages. It was about the Allagash Village veterans of World War II. But to her it was about her brother.

"My brother was the only boy from here to die in the war." She offered it to me to look at. It was opened to the page with her brother's picture on it. On the opposite page was a picture of the U.S.S. *Wasp,* which had been sunk off the coast of Guadalcanal, taking him with it. I told her my father had been on shore there with the Marines.

The air was over-warm and stale, as if the windows were rarely opened and everything within had sat without moving for too long. I regretted later not having lingered longer for her and for me, but after three days and nights in the thin, clear air of the outdoors the place felt stifling and I had it in my mind to get on the road as soon as possible. So I thanked her and left.

Jim Stang will put me down on Umsaskis Lake and fly away taking every bit of sound with him. From there it's about fifty three miles to Allagash Village and Mrs. McBraierty's house. Other than forest rangers' cabins (3), there is not another human dwelling for at least forty miles in any direction. The Allagash River is deep within the heart of the Maine wilderness, ten million uninhabited acres, an area larger than Belgium and the largest uninhabited forest in the lower forty-eight states. And all only a few hundred miles north of Boston.

You get to a certain age and fall into a particular demographic and you begin to receive distinctive junk mail. My daughter is 16 and now gets two or three letters from colleges a day, along with free fashion magazines and record club offers. Soon she will be getting solicitations from the armed forces and credit card companies. My wife and I are deluged with high-end credit card offers and home refinancing pitches.

About seven or eight years ago I began to receive ads from adventure travel companies. They would come brilliantly packaged. In some cases they hit you with part of their message before you even opened the envelope, a good idea considering how seldom I open unsolicited ads. Emblazoned diagonally across the front of the oversized package might be a line like, "Hike the deep primordial forests of Borneo!" in some vibrant electrifying script, or sometimes a spectacular scene, say of a Himalayan trail into a Shangri-la type valley, covers the surface of the envelope. You have to open it. I began to become intrigued. I would love to hike in the Himalayas, I thought. I sent away for one company's catalog of trips. This of course put me on every adventure tour mailing list. Good! I was getting serious about the idea. I have always been attracted to the stories and to the experiences of expeditions into strange lands. I have loved the tales of explorers. *The Journals of Lewis and Clark* edited by Bernard DeVoto remains the only book I have ever read twice.

As a child my brothers and I sometimes would leave our home during a heavy rain or snow announcing to our parents, "We're going on an expedition!" Bad weather conditions, cabin fever, and our fevered imaginations propelled us. Our parents were not at all hesitant to let us leave. In retrospect, I wonder about the meaning of that. In any case off we'd go in a line through deep snow or torrential rain, the only kids out, into the woods imagining ourselves to be Rogers' Rangers. If weather conditions were more favorable and offered inadequate impediments we would make up for it by choosing the most difficult route available, through thick growths of thorn bushes or swamps. I know of no other children who "played" this way. Play it was. We were transported by it, our imaginations enlivened by the real-life feel of it. Other kids from the neighborhood didn't understand. Sometimes a few would come along attracted to the sound of it. "An expedition! Great. Where are we going?" Usually they would turn back miserable, angry, and defensive or else continue on to avoid disgrace, miserable, disgruntled, and struggling for comprehension. The Currans were weird kids in many ways.

A difficult journey through an alien environment has long held strong appeal for me. It touches directly upon very old and deep desires. These adventure trips sounded like a pretty cool expedition to me. I wanted to do it. My wife listened patiently with heroic neutrality as I brought out the world atlas and thought out loud about my plans. The question was, where? Time and cost whittled down the range of choices. A trip to the Himalayas or anywhere in Asia would cost several thousand dollars and require that I be gone for weeks. Out of the question. I couldn't take myself or that kind of money out of my family just for me. Next, I thought of South America. It's closer, has jungles, mountains, wild and unexplored areas. I honed in on a trip to Chile. Two weeks, river rafting, volcano climbing to 10,000 feet, jungle hiking and half the price of any of the Asian trips. I still have a lot of little kid in me and as with little kids my enthusiasms and impulses can be somewhat immoderate. I can picture myself there. My imagination is vivid, a virtual experience needing only the light touch of a color brochure to activate it. I do however return to reality once the show is over. This trip also was just too much. Not fair to the family, though kindly, no one ever told me so.

Sometime in 1996 I received a mailing from Sunrise County Canoe Expeditions out of Grove Post, Maine. They are river guides who offer canoe trips all over North America, including the far north of Canada, Iceland, and the American West. This really got my attention.

I like the look of things from a river. Even in settled regions, it provides a fresh view of the land and a chance to catch silent peeks at wildlife in their own homes—herons, hawks, turtles, muskrats. I had paddled stretches of the Concord and Assabet Rivers in central Massachusetts. These are flatwater streams that run through forest and farmland, backyards and golf courses. The Concord flows under the Old North Bridge and canoeing to it is a popular school field trip. I have rented canoes in central Florida at a place called De Leon Springs, where a branch of the St. Johns River begins. There you can paddle among the alligators. Sightings are pretty common. Sometimes when people capsize they are not eaten.

One afternoon I was on the river with my wife and 10-year-old son. Kevin was in the bow. Pat lounged like Cleopatra in the middle. We spotted a young alligator lying in watery grass near the riverbank.

"Hey let's get over there and take some pictures," I said. We coasted toward it.

"A little closer," I whispered. We carefully dipped our paddles in the murky brown water and quietly pushed ourselves a little further. Pat had already begun snapping pictures.

"A little closer," I said. Kevin went to put his paddle in the water then stopped and turned to me.

"Daddy, we probably shouldn't go too close. What if its mother is nearby?"

"Okaaaay. Backward," I agreed. My enthusiasms aren't usually dangerous, but occasionally better judgment has to come to me from external sources such as small children or three-foot waves in ice-cold rivers.

Twice I participated in a canoe race. It's a big prize money race for 10 percent of the participants. For the rest it is merely a waterborne melee to the swarming bars downriver. It's the River Rat Canoe Race, held every year on the first Saturday in April. It is a seven-mile run on fast to nonexistent current (no white water) from Athol to Orange, Massachusetts, on the Millers River. There are often nearly 400 canoes entered. It is the highlight of the year for these two slightly shabby, all but forgotten, former mill towns. Their Mardi Gras. On the water it's a combination chariot race and roller derby, generously seasoned with alcohol before, during, and after the race, except for that aforementioned 10 percent who zip out with serious faces in their handmade, dagger-sharp, scull-like devices, paddling and grunting with machine-like precision. Leaving the cretins (the other 90 percent) behind at the start howling, waving paddles in the air and gleefully cruising over the bobbing heads of the fallen. Once I went to the real Mardi Gras in New Orleans as a member of my college rugby team. We were there ostensibly for a tournament. But everyone from every team understood that the tournament was secondary and no more than an excuse to be there for the parties. Then the team from the Citadel showed up. Now this was 1972 and we northerners were a shaggy lot and undisciplined even for rugby players. These guys came onto the Tulane campus (where all the teams gathered) like red-necked versions of the Hitler Youth. They wore matching bright red warm-up jackets and pants, shaved heads 20 years before their time and, most disturbing, they were jogging. In a long line of twos they chugged in chanting some warrior hymn and looking, to us, like fools. The serious canoeists reminded me of those guys.

It was fun. But twice was enough. I'd gone twice and not tipped over. Any more than that seemed to be foolishly pushing my luck. Besides, I sensed that canoeing could be something more than that.

I have always liked the feel of a canoe. The way it soundlessly and almost effortlessly moves through water. I like the history in it; the fact that Indians did it and taught it to us. We have a large pond a quarter mile walk through the woods behind our house. My wife and I had talked occasionally of the fun it would be to canoe around in it. Maybe go up the stream that feeds into it. It's a nice area. Conservation land. No homes or development of any kind. There are great blue herons back there, snakes, turtles, deer, and even some beavers. But we never did anything about it until the Christmas of 1994.

We decided to buy a canoe and surprise the kids with it. I knew nothing at all about canoes beyond the minimum in making it go. I drove out to the New Hampshire border and picked up a blue, 16-foot matted fiberglass Nature Bound (later to be referred to as "that cheap no-good canoe"), including three paddles and four life jackets for about $500, had it tied onto the top of my car, drove home at dusk and parked in the woods near my house. I told the kids the car was at the gas station. That night I snuck the canoe into our basement, which has a large walk-in barn type door. No one goes in our basement. It is poorly lit. The ceiling of exposed wooden joists is clouded with cobwebs which hang like Spanish moss all about. There are ancient tools, rusted heavy chains, farmer's implements, lots of scimitar-like old scythe blades, long pike-like iceman tools and, with its high ceiling and old fieldstone walls, it has very much the look and feel of a medieval dungeon, where bad things have happened. The secret of the canoe was safe down there.

Late at night on Christmas Eve I brought it around and through the front door and laid it down in the living room. It was a big hit the next morning. It was 60 degrees that Christmas day. We carried it down to the pond and paddled around through a skim coat of ice. It was a great time. The following week I received the material from Sunrise Expeditions. Canoeing was to be the thing.

I picked out a trip to the Soper River on Baffin Island in Canada's Northwest Territory. Sunrise described it as "the ultimate northern canoe trip: about as far north as you can go and still find 'running water!'" The Soper Valley "features some of the earth's most spectacular and dramatic glacial Arctic landscape." Inuit guides would serve as an accompaniment. Trips were eight days long and cost $1,850, air fare not included.

This sounded like something worth doing. I immediately began telling people of my plans. Then I told Walter Bickford. Walter is a neighbor of mine and a real outdoorsman. He had been for several years Massachusetts' Commissioner of Fisheries and Wildlife under Governor

Dukakis in the 1980s. He has hunted, hiked, and canoed all over the United States and Canada and is a well-known nature and river systems expert. In short, we had little in common other than our sons who had been friends since nursery school.

He said, "I hope you like mosquitoes."

"Huh?" was about all I could muster for a stopped-dead-in-my-tracks response.

He chuckled, "Oh, there'll be plenty of mosquitoes and flies up there," and proceeded to enlighten me regarding the desperate voracity of the flying sharks of the North where huge numbers congregate in the short season they have available and their lively response to the slim pickings available to them, which in this case would include me. Walter has spent a good deal of time in Alaska and, I had to believe, knew what he was talking about. He chuckled throughout and as I listened I went sort of limp. Then he asked me why I hadn't considered Maine. Maine? All I knew about Maine had to do with people's inexplicable desire to drive three hours to a 24-hour, seven-day-a-week store called L. L. Bean, water too cold to swim in, and jokes about drunken lumberjacks marrying their sisters. I had been raised in a Cape Cod family and never had any use for Maine. Up until then I had been there only twice, at night, to Portland to play football.

Walter wishes he had been born over a hundred years ago. He barely tolerated the 20th century. The interior of his home is all hand-oiled pine. It has wide plank floors. Everything is an aged dark brown. There is a cast-iron wood-burning stove for cooking and a wood-burning stove for heat. The lighting is dim, giving it a candlelit feel where shadows thrive. The smell of smoke is faintly present all the time. The skull of a black bear sits on his old oak filing cabinet. A bear skin, mounted antlers, and bighorn sheep horns adorn his living room walls. The tools of the rifle and bow hunter are visible here and there. The book shelves which cover half of the wall space in the living room are filled with books on nature, Indians, the pioneer and woodsman's life, and the tales of the mountain men, Walter's true heroes. He is a small man with the body of a middleweight and a face shaped as if carved from wood. He looks like an Indian with a white man's complexion. He is the dominant presence in the physical home if not the spiritual one; a discontented curmudgeon born too late for the life he needs. People love him or hate him. His wife and kids love him but take every opportunity to remind him what a crank he is.

He brought me inside and laid open his ragged copy of the *Maine Gazetteer*. The cover was detached and the corners of all the pages had curled and were smudged with the tea-colored smears of repeated use.

"How about the Moose River trip, the Bow Trip? That's a nice trip. Gail! When did we do Moose River?" He ignored her response. "That's a nice trip. A lot of moose out there. You don't need a shuttle. You put in here at Attean Pond. [Actually a lake nearly 5 miles across. It takes a lot for a body of water to impress Maine enough to deserve the label of lake.] Go across here. Portage over to Holeb Pond. Bit of a carry [1 1/4 miles!]. Then you pick up the Moose River out of Holeb and it'll take you right on back into Attean. And you end up right back where you started. Route takes the shape of a bow. It's the Bow Trip. Takes about three days." He told me I should get the AMC *Maine River Guide*. I picked up a new *Maine Gazetteer* as well that very day.

From that day forward Maine has looked entirely different to me. Some guys there might still marry their sisters and cousins and have three-eyed children. So what. I also began to learn of its wilderness. I read everything I could get my hands on. Books on solo canoe camping, wilderness canoeing, and Maine rivers began piling up in my home office. South America and Baffin Island became irrelevant with the great Maine wilderness rivers right next door. And if Walter was impressed by it, which he surely was, who was I not to be.

"Few river trips in Maine can guarantee the diversity of the Moose River Bow Trip as it passes through a remote niche of northwestern Maine," says the DeLorme *Maine Geographic River Guide*, Volume II. The trip offers lake and quiet river paddling with only a couple of short Class II rapids. The area is thick with moose. Sightings are common. "Beginners and experts alike can appreciate the river's wildness, its striking scenery and abundance of wildlife." A three-day trip is the norm for this thirty-four-mile circuit. This sounded just right as my introduction to Maine wilderness canoeing.

V

CLEAR DRY AIR HAD BLOWN INTO THE MOOSE RIVER REGION FROM the west the night before kicking out the heavy heat and humidity of the days before. Attean Pond, the first of the two lakes I planned to cross that day, lay before me deep blue and beautiful under a matching sky. Small islands rose dark green like shaggy pyramids from its surface. The water was smooth. Only a light breeze could be felt. I hurried to get ready. The put-in was a deep flat beach. Not a single mosquito buzzed near. I was in the water by 10:00 A.M. and had seen my first moose by 10:15. A young female was browsing among the water grass near the shore. A hawk circled overhead. Loons bobbed on the water, their sharply defined black and white markings distinctive even from a distance. I cut through the water with energy and an anticipation stoked to a bright glow by the quick rewards it had already received. But by 10:45 I was in trouble.

Attean Pond is 4³/₄ miles across and shaped like a funnel with the narrow end facing due west. It hides a demon in its spout which cannot be felt by the preparing traveler starting at the northeast corner of the wide end of the funnel in the protected nook of the beach. After photographing the moose, I stayed in near the shore hoping to see more. As I rounded a house-sized boulder the wind caught me. My canoe was poorly balanced, the bow sitting up too high. The wind yanked it to the left, away from the shore, threatening to turn me broadside to the white-capped waves now bashing against my boat. I had entered the chute. Strong winds blowing west to east were channeled between the mountains and roared up the spout of the funnel that was Attean Pond. White spray blew hard in shredded streams off the tops of the waves. I had a new broad-blade paddle and I wasn't used to it. It carried a lot of water and it took all my strength in every stroke to pull it back. I had to paddle as fast as I could to have any chance of controlling the bow against the wind and waves. Sometimes the pressure on the blade was too great and it turned in my hand, wasting the stroke. It was too much for me. I circled around counterclockwise and came in behind the boulder again and out of the wind. I tried it again. Same result. The wind kept taking the bow of my boat out with it to the middle of the lake where the wind and waves were highest. In addition, I was being swept backwards.

I should have seen all this from a distance. It was there to be seen even from the calmer waters which preceded it. I should have known to balance my boat. But I was ignorant and did not know how to look and see.

Experienced canoeists know about lakes and their dangers. They have the sense to wait out the wind, to pull over and let it go by. They cross in early morning, dusk, and even in moonlit nights, times when strong winds usually go slack. That weekend two canoeists capsized and drowned in Moosehead Lake just to the north.

It was clear I couldn't beat that wind, especially alone. I'd been lucky to escape it twice. But stopping and waiting, even camping in the lee of the giant boulder on that sunny, sheltered, bug-free, stony beach never even entered my mind. I hadn't the experience or the instincts for such sensibility. I'll walk it through, I thought. Must keep moving forward after all. So for the next three or four miles I walked my canoe through the water along the shore in depths from knee to neck high, once swimming through a deep section around a rock, canoe in hand. All afternoon, splashing my way along, all the way to the end of Attean Pond.

It took about four hours. Several times I tried to get back in and paddle and had to give it up and get back in the water and onto the slippery rocks which covered the bottom from one end of the lake to the

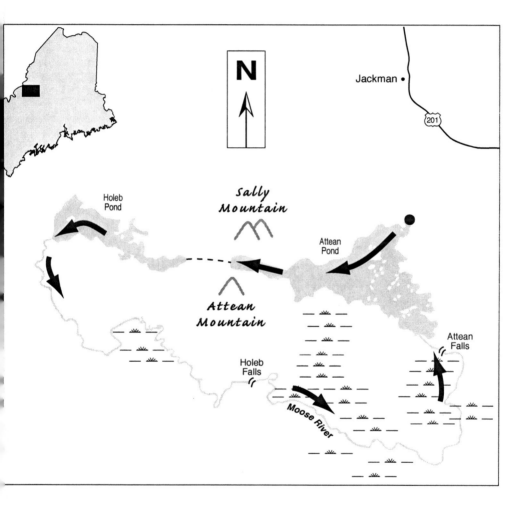

N

Jackman •

201

Holeb
Pond

*Sally
Mountain*

Attean
Pond

*Attean
Mountain*

Attean
Falls

Holeb
Falls

Moose River

other. Topographical maps only show you the shape and size of lakes. On maps all lakes are still and flat. They cannot show you the winds and waves which are more deadly than white water to the open canoe.

I reached the shore. Miraculously I hadn't sprained an ankle, but my knee ached. A bald eagle curved through the peaceful sky overhead, the first I had ever seen in my life and I didn't care. I had a 1¼-mile portage ahead of me and I needed to rest. I took four ibuprofen and lay down for a while.

During the weeks preceding the trip I had thought a lot about this long carry and thought that I had outsmarted it. I had made a type of cart out of two 14-inch inflatable wheelbarrow tires, a ³/4-inch steel tube (as an axle), a sawed off hockey stick and duct tape. With this canoe-bearing vehicle I could bring over the whole load in one trip. I would simply walk, with one hand holding up the bow end of the canoe, the cart supporting the rear third, striding majestically and leisurely along the grassy path, all the way to Holeb Pond—the envy of all who saw me.

The rest and the medicine restored me. While I recuperated another party arrived. Six taciturn Scandinavians of some sort in two large aluminum canoes landed nearby and without a word began unloading for the carry. They ignored me.

I got up and began erecting my cart which I had carried in pieces in the bow. A couple of them glanced my way expressionlessly. They must be jealous, I thought, and too envious to show it. They don't seem to be very nice people. They should be over here by my side congratulating me on my invention. I worked proudly. This was going to be great.

They were down the trail and out of sight by the time I rolled off the beach and into the woods. All my gear was in the canoe. Mercifully there were no eyewitnesses to the debacle. The trimmed green boulevards I had allowed myself to imagine, having neglected of course to actually ask anyone what the path was like, did not exist. I had not gone thirty yards before I had to give it up. The cart that is, not the walk. I still had the walk. And now I would have an extra twenty pounds to carry. The trail was in most places far too narrow for the 2½-foot width of my cart. It was often very steep or very swampy and in a dozen ways completely prevented me from living out my glorious scheme. I realize

44

now that the Scandinavians were appraising me with contempt or pity rather than envy. It had been such a big hit in my backyard.

Back and forth I went, $6\frac{1}{4}$ miles in all before I had all my gear to the campsite on Holeb Pond and the sun went down. A full day of nearly nonstop traveling, most of it on foot, had brought me six miles. And I was still miles from the Moose River.

The wind blew rough and noisy in uneven gusts all night and kept me awake with its ominous portent. What if it continued into the next day? How would I cross that next lake? I couldn't walk it again. It still hadn't occurred to me to simply wait.

I am not a great sleeper in unfamiliar settings. I sleep in short snatches sprinkled through the night, an hour or two at a time, more aware of being awake than of having been asleep. So I'm always surprised by the sudden appearance of the sun. It is the only proof that I have been asleep.

I woke to a bright sun and . . . silence. The wind had stopped. The trees stood still. The lake below me was flat, motionless, waiting. I skipped breakfast, loaded up fast, jumped in, and paddled as fast as I could, fearing the wind might rise again at any moment. It didn't. But I think that it was there that the dread was born.

It was a wonderful trip. I had the aforementioned encounter with the charging moose, the mystery visitor at the second campsite on the grassy bank, and finished with an easy early morning return crossing of a quiet Attean Pond. Yet I never lost the low hum of unpleasant possibilities; the sense that something could go seriously and unexpectedly wrong at any moment and that I was on my own against it.

As I crossed Attean Pond under a lifting fog that anxious sensation rose to full consciousness. It was August and the water level was low. Stumps and rocks which at higher water would have been safely covered, instead crouched silently inches below the surface. The day before I had been knocked right out of my canoe by a submerged rock I had not seen. I put on my life jacket and began to actively imagine the worst. I twitched at the touch of every breeze for the whole of the two-hour crossing.

The sight of the beach, the flat man-made look of it, the shining cars and trucks parked there and the tiny human figures moving about had an exhilarating effect on me. My joy grew as the distance closed and I finished with bursting pride and a smile I couldn't and wouldn't wipe away.

Others were preparing for canoe trips of their own. My canoe crunched to a stop and I hopped out half expecting a reception or at least some acknowledgment and a few questions. Two fit-looking women were packing up, intent upon their business. A grandfather with a vintage wood and canvas Old Town looked to be taking grandchildren on a day trip. He nodded. That was fine. My happiness was undiminished and that, among other things, is what has always brought me back and what I try to keep in mind in dreary and dreadful times. The next two trips I took the following spring, the ill-fated Seboeis River trip and Son of Seboeis, solidified my unwanted partnership with fear and loathing in Maine. But the memory of that landing at the end of the Moose River trip and others like it, in the end, always wins out, and in the winter I read and plan and prepare. And when I go to bed at night, many nights, in the pitch black of my bedroom, I close my eyes and I try to imagine I am in the woods along a riverside, alone and happy.

VI

I ROSE BEFORE MY ALARM, AT 3:30 A.M. IT WAS FRIDAY, JUNE 23, THE DAY of my departure for the Allagash. I did not feel tired. Nor did I feel excitement or enthusiasm. Instead I felt a kind of dreary evenness between well-spaced flashes of anxiety. I had intended to pay close attention to everything around and in me as I prepared to leave and as I traveled north, my sensory antenna way up to catch observations and sensations of use to this book I was writing. But as I packed quietly in the deep dark among my sleeping family I felt nothing. I pulled out of my driveway into the empty street with no sense of drama or expectation. I drove north beside a rising sun and under a brightening sky and by the time I reached Portland the sky was turning blue and it was time for my first stop and then, my tapes.

I had not anticipated them. I hadn't chosen them. Yet since I began making trips to Maine three years ago specific rituals have formed. They emerged naturally as any ritual should. Their meanings are obscure at best but I adhere to them lovingly. I look forward to their fulfillment along the way. The first is the obligatory stop at the Route 95 Burger King just before Portland, about 1 hour 45 minutes from home. I stop whether or not I am hungry or thirsty. I will become hungry and thirsty regardless. It is a conditioned response. I like my caffeine in the form of a cold carbonated drink, even at 5:30 A.M., so I know I'll enjoy the

Coke. I will also get a Croissandwich, to go. Same thing every time. It's the only time I ever eat one.

I park and check the bungees, which hold down the canoe, make sure everything is snug and as it should be. A few cars are in the parking lot, and a few more are coming and going. Solo truckers, people in pairs and small groups, families, are walking slowly to and from the Burger King. The adults are hobbling along, working out the kinks from a long period of sitting. The children move sleepily, leaning against their parents' hips. Teens slouch sullenly along. Nobody speaks much above a whisper, if at all. It is quiet.

I feel different from all of them and imagine that they can see it. I am not on my way to what any of them are on their way to and I sense they know it in some dim way. On another level I realize they are oblivious and couldn't care less. The over-cool air-conditioning chills me the moment I enter. I hate it. It makes me feel I have a cold coming on and I can't wait to get out.

I ride on cruise control nearly all the way and I know it can make me drive badly, lazily weaving in and out of traffic in an effort to keep from using the brake or the accelerator. A half hour earlier I'd cut off a trucker on the Portsmouth Bridge. Never saw him. He was furious at me. He caught up to me and hung out his window screaming at me. He was mean and ugly and looked like the trucker in *Thelma and Louise*. He was right. I deserved it. But how could I apologize in pantomime at seventy miles an hour? As I stood in line waiting to place my order it occurred to me that the trucker might stop here as well. He'd pull into the parking lot and recognize my truck. I could picture him entering the Burger King: big stomach, big hairy arms, greasy red baseball cap upon an unshaven face sitting on a short thick neck, his red eyes darting about looking for me. Was I going to have to fight this guy? My order came and I got out quick, scanning the parking lot warily.

Back in the truck I lay my Croissandwich out on the seat next to me, on top of the bag which I flattened. The napkin is placed right next to it. I pull out onto the highway. I don't take a bite of food until I have settled back into cruise control. I love to eat and drive. They go together so beautifully. I only wish it could last longer. I do now and have always

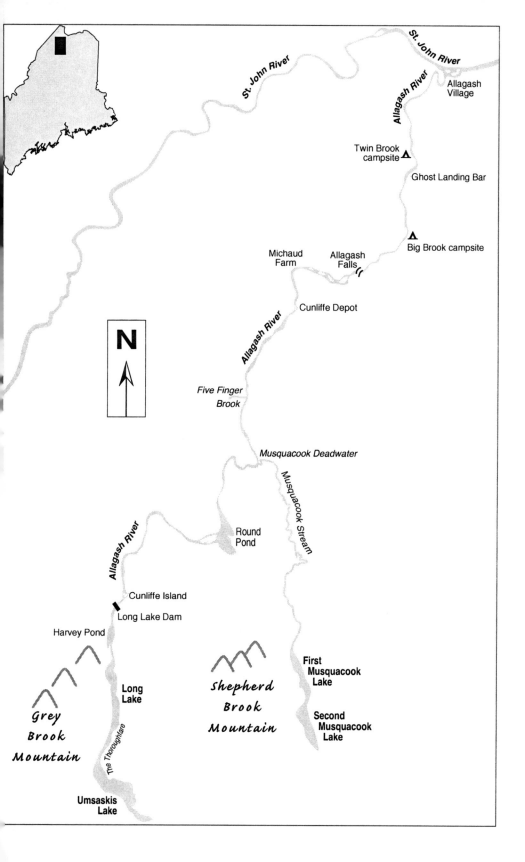

eaten way too fast. I try especially hard to go slow here but I no sooner finish chewing and swallowing a bite than I am drawn back by that warm salty aftertaste and I am compelled, far too soon, to pick it up again and take another bite.

I have a friend who is an alcoholic. He quit drinking a long time ago. He said the hardest thing to give up, and the memory that is most blissful to him, was driving along drinking a beer. For him they just went together and I know what he means.

It is a long way to any river worth doing in Maine and when you ride alone sound is your only companion. I have my routines there as well. I carry familiar radio stations as far as I can. I can hold Massachusetts stations until about the Maine border. But that's a small fraction of the trip; only 70 minutes out of at least seven hours, more or less. Then I'll pick up the Portland stations, which aren't bad. I can carry them for about another 45 minutes. That leaves four to seven hours to fill. Only then will I begin to play tapes. I buy them just for this leg of the trip. And I never, under any circumstances, play them at any other time during the year. They are only played between Portland and Millinocket or Vanceboro or Jackman or Fort Kent. I can't afford to get sick of this music and I quickly would if I allowed myself to listen to it any old time I wanted. I cannot let that happen. The tapes are all that separates me from the grim landscape of northern Maine radio; a thin barrier between my brain and theirs. I like to peek though, take dips into that world.

It is comprised of four things. First, is the terminal blandness of very mainstream brand name pop. Every song is one you've heard a billion times before. Nothing but the hits. The DJs are all deep-affected-voiced caricatures of DJs who are at their worst when trying to be witty. The best parts of their programming are the local ads. They at least tell you something about the community you are passing through, something indigenous and sort of real. Whereas the music comes from a package sent out from some national headquarters, chosen by guys whom I imagine look like insurance salesman, based on data which are as lifeless as actuarial tables and certainly have not been influenced by aesthetics or intellect. Some guy from a Bangor station cut Dylan's *Positively Fourth*

Street short at about two and a half minutes, for a meat ad. I can never linger here long.

Second, are the country and western stations. They take up more and more of the utilized airspace the farther north you go. All it is, as far as I can tell, is bad electrified pop with an accent. There's nothing country or western or traditional about it. None of it, for instance, is acoustic anymore. "Pure Country!" they say, but it sure ain't pure. It all sounds lavishly produced, high tech, enhanced, reinforced, over-dubbed and a far far cry from a lonesome country girl on a stage with a microphone and a wooden guitar.

But I always give it a try. I hear about Shania Twain and Garth Brooks and I'm curious to hear what they sound like and what all the fuss is about. I saw Shania Twain on TV on some awards show in a tiny black leather skirt, thigh-high black boots with five-inch heels and what I think was a black corset, traditional backwoods ho-down garb, and so I get her. But I don't get Garth Brooks. I hear nothing distinctive in his sound, melodies, or voice and his lyrics sound just like most country lyrics, simple, literal, and mundane. And he's dull looking. He seems like a nice guy though because he loves playing baseball and is humble about it.

Finally, there are the Bible stations and the dull buzz of empty space. I was driving home from Allagash Village last summer, at 6:00 A.M. on a Saturday. As I drove up to Fort Kent to catch Route 11 for the long ride south, I searched the dial for something local. Later I asked people at home, "How many separate stations do you suppose you could count on the FM dial from one end to the other if you go real slow and try to catch them all?" Thirty? Forty? Between Allagash and Fort Kent I found five stations, all French. The rest, dead air. So I bring tapes.

I have three Bruce Springsteen tapes, *Greetings from Asbury Park, The River*, and this short one with only about four songs on it, all live, including Dylan's "Chimes of Freedom," which is why I bought it. I have the Stones' 1970 live *Get Yer Ya's Ya's Out!*, Grateful Dead's *American Beauty*, The Clash (a minor mistake), John Prine's *Greatest Hits*, and Dylan's *Biograph*, which someone gave me right before I left.

The music helps, especially Springsteen. It gives me strength against the dread, which had been tapping away at me, all the way.

There were clear skies in every direction all the way to Millinocket. The forecast had been for partly cloudy skies, chance of scattered thunderstorms for the first two days. These skies looked better than that. I began to feel lucky.

But as I turned off the highway onto the east to west road to Katahdin Air, I began to notice the treetops bending and the leaves on the oaks and maples flipping over to show their pale green bottoms. The wind here was strong. And it was coming out of the north, maybe northwest, precisely the direction I would be heading.

I arrived early as I always do and checked in. Through the big picture window in the office you could see whitecaps flickering on the big lake in the distance outside the sheltered cove. Waves splashed white against a rocky island. I don't like to see the color white on a lake.

On my last trip down the Allagash I'd seen a couple of canoes with small motors attached. I'd been shocked and strongly disapproved. I was surprised they were allowed and surprised Allagash travelers would even want to use one. I thought they would be a pure breed of wilderness canoeists. I guessed they had used them to help cross the giant lakes to the south—Chamberlain, Eagle, and Churchill—but still it wasn't right. The voyageurs used no motors. Lewis and Clark went 2,000 miles against the current without motors. The sound of engines should not be brought into this wilderness.

I asked the woman in the office if I could rent a motor.

"We're all out. None left," she smiled.

"Heard any weather?" I asked.

"No, but here comes Jim," she bobbed her chin up toward the window behind me. "He'll know."

A small red and white single-engine floatplane was circling in for a landing. You couldn't hear it. The wind was blowing the sound away. He cut his engine and coasted smoothly up to the dock, then hopped out and secured bow and stern lines. He unloaded a film crew from Maine TV Channel Six. We nodded to each other. I introduced myself to Jim, a short nimble fellow of about forty with a surprisingly smooth face for someone who's outside up here as much as he is. He looked more like a science teacher than a grizzled wilderness pilot, and a world apart from the banged up pilot and shuttle driver from the Seboeis River.

"I'm early," I said sort of apologetically.

"Well, I got to gas up and such. You got a canoe?" He was squinting at the canoe at my feet.

"Yeah. I have all my own stuff. Don't need to rent anything. I wondered about a motor but I guess there's none left."

He spat out a grunt of disgust. "They're all beat to shit. People." He didn't continue. "We're gonna have to wait see if this wind dies down. I was just pushing against a head wind. Had my speedometer reading 120, with my actual speed being 75 knots. And with a canoe strapped to my side." He shook his head.

"Is the wind out of the north?" I asked, expectantly.

"Oh yeah. We'll get you up though," and off he went to attend to business. I sat and waited outside watching him go back and forth.

A pal of his stopped by. They got to talking about the goings on about the lake.

"That eagle still nesting out around the point, top a that dead tree?" the friend asked.

"Yep," Jim replied. "Two little ones in the nest."

"You know that loon's nest out the island got swamped by a wave, took the chicks right out the nest. I seen she's rebuilt the nest further up the rocks."

"Hey, an eagle came down last week and plucked a baby loon right off a this dock. Swoosh!" Jim made a sweeping motion with his arm.

"I saw a snapping turtle once reach up and pull a chick off a log. Just pulled it under."

They paused a moment to reflect upon the splendid cruelty of nature. They were standing on the dock near the shore facing the lake about fifteen feet from me.

Jim continued, "Jeez, I came around the shed t' other day and started hearin' the most God awful racket, honkin' and splashin' and it was two loons mating. I thought they were killing each other." I laughed and they half turned and smiled at me.

"Yeah and mallards are the same way," Jim's friend added. "The male'll hold the female right under the water and peck the hell out the back of her neck!"

I chuckled. "Boy I don't know why anybody bothers to go up the Allagash with all that's going on right here."

Jim's pal laughed, "Yeah, but that's all's happened here the past two months."

"It's dying down a bit," Jim said, speaking of the wind. "Let's go."

I sure wanted to believe him. I had about eleven miles of lake and open water to cross, heading north. I wanted to believe in anything that would lessen the torment which might await me.

I hadn't enjoyed my last flight in this small plane and I didn't enjoy this one either. Though I sit nearly shoulder to shoulder to the pilot, conversation is virtually impossible unless you want to yell. But I wasn't air sick. I am here to tell you that those Sea-Bands you wear around your wrists with the little nodules sewn in to put pressure on the inside of the wrist do work. We bumped around quite a bit but I felt not even a flutter of nausea. And I was looking for it. The absence of motion sickness left me free to look around and think of other things. I tried to figure out what at least one of the scores of gauges and dials on his dashboard meant but failed. I studied the ground beneath us, noting the different shades of green as signs of different types of trees or stages of reforestation. I noticed the logging roads, the only means of travel for wheeled vehicles for a hundred miles. Most looked abandoned and in the process of being retaken by the forest. These were dim green lanes winding short distances through the woods. Others still carried the dirt-colored double parallel lines of regular or at least semi-regular vehicular travel. These would be used by loggers and hunters. Finally there were the main logging roads, one or two straight sand-colored tracks extending for many miles up and over hills and around lakes, the main arteries of logging transport in the Great North Woods. The others I have mentioned were the veins and capillaries off of these routes. None of them is paved and the secondary and tertiary roads can be terribly pitted so that you have to crawl along at about 5 miles per hour. On the least used, branches reach out from both sides to take away your view and give your vehicle a real good scraping. You don't want to bring your Jaguar down one.

The mark of Man is clearly upon the land up there. It is not an untouched or unexplored wilderness. Yet in an hour of flight time, passing over maybe 500 square miles of territory, not a single vehicle could be seen and the roof of only a single dwelling was present. That being the roof of the ranger cabin at the start of the Allagash River at the outlet of Churchill Lake. There are no stores, neighborhoods, or street signs, no paved roads or sidewalks, no telephone poles, phone lines, or cell phone towers, no electricity except that which can be supplied by a gas-powered generator. The ancient water avenues of lake, pond, river, and stream are touched least of all by the past or current presence of Man. With only three dams remaining along the waterway—Telos, Lock Dam, and Churchill Dam—the river flows much the same as it has for the thousands of years since the last ice age.

During the heyday of the 19th and early 20th century logging boom, numerous dams raised the level of the large lakes, Eagle, Churchill, and Chamberlain, while limiting their release of water to the north-flowing Allagash. By means of a ferocious energy, the keenest of Yankee ingenuity and the limitless power of greed, lumber barons succeeded in sending all that water south instead, carrying billions of feet of timber over flooded streams and blasted channels and canals to the south-running Penobscot, away from Canada and down to Bangor, at that time, the lumber capital of the world. Meanwhile small-time American loggers from north Aroostook County and Canadians from the St. John would see their north-bound log drives run aground in the artificially shallow waters of the Allagash. When that happened, angry loggers sometimes took matters into their own hands, jumping into canoes or bateaux and heading south to the Churchill Lake dams, forcing open and spiking the gates, sending some of that "Bangor" water flowing north again to lift their logs, the fruit of a full winter's backbreaking labor, to the St. John's mills.

In July of 1905 Aroostook loggers Arthur Brown and Bill Cunliffe, Jr., had their timber jam up in the low water channels above Round Pond on the Allagash—a 2-mile stretch of wood lying useless and immobile. Brown and Cunliffe paddled up to Eagle Lake and hiked cross country to the Lock Dam on Churchill Lake. Armed watchmen often guarded the site. The two loggers crept in close. It was midsummer, late for log driving, and only a single man had been left to guard the dam. The two loggers hurried back downriver to report to the drive boss John Sweeney. Sweeney took five men and fifty sticks of dynamite down to Eagle Lake and up the dry stream bed which led to the Lock Dam. While a couple of loggers posed as hunters and lured the guard away with hunting stories, others entered his cabin, threw away his rifle, and planted dynamite in the giant gates. The guard could only watch help-lessly as the dam was blasted and the lake's waters rushed through. Sweeney was later arrested but a local judge soon released him. He never came to trial.

Victories were short-lived however, and the spigot was always quickly turned off again. Nothing but the gasoline engine would end that stolen northern flow.

When Thoreau traveled this way in the 1850s the raised water level in the flooded lakes had killed off all the trees which had grown along the old waterline creating a dramatically altered and forbidding envi-ronment.

"A belt of dead trees stood all around the lake, some far out in the water, with the others prostrate behind them, and they made the shore, for the most part, almost inaccessible. This is the effect of the dam at the outlet. Thus the natural sandy or rocky shore, with its green fringe, was concealed and destroyed."

Timber has long since ceased to be transported by water, so most of the old dams have been breached and the ones that remain allow the lakes to feed the Allagash again so that it flows as it did for the Indians and as it did before the Indians came.

As I looked down upon the countless lakes and ponds, I was not thinking of any of this. I was brooding over those white specks scattered across those vast landscapes of blue and the long white streamers which crossed them in straight lines north to south. I was preparing myself for the possibility of spending my first day camped on the shore without ever even getting into my canoe.

VII

WE SWOOPED IN FOR A LANDING ON UMSASKIS LAKE. IT IS A PENOBSCOT
phrase meaning "place having opposite points which run out to meet
one another," which I don't really understand unless water sometimes
backflows from Long Lake just to the north, sending water flowing in
from the Allagash. It is shaped like a loose S with points on either end by
which the river enters and departs. It is not a large lake, only being about
three miles across. It is surrounded by low hills covered in varied shades
of green. Light green alders trace the rocky shore while the black-green
spruce and firs stand tightly pressed behind and climb the sides of hills in
every direction. The logging road called American Realty Road crosses
the waterway up at the lake's outlet. It is a dirt road but well built and
maintained. Heavily loaded and overloaded 22-wheeler logging trucks
barrel along it at fearless speeds, throwing out clouds of dust, rocks, and a
forceful wave of air to either side. It's their road, bought and paid for, and
if you're on it and see one coming you're obliged to get out of the way.
You pull over as you would for a fire truck and you don't mind because
you don't want to pass anywhere near one.

There is a ranger station there at the bridge. But there is a very
remote feel to this lake. The ranger lives here alone during the summer
in a log cabin. In winter she moves down to Churchill Dam. There was
once a logging camp on the site of the ranger station. Before that,

Maliseet Indians fished and hunted the region, which is still plentiful
with moose, deer, bear, fish, and waterfowl. They camped along its shores
during the hunt before packing up and heading north, downriver to
their villages. The Umsaskis may have been the southern limit of their
lands. It was a fluid boundary shared with the Penobscots. Whites know
it by its Penobscot name because Penobscot guides from the south first
brought whites to it and gave them their name for it.

The Maliseet, sometimes spelled Malecite or Malacite, called themselves "people of the beautiful river." That river is the St. John and the
country it travels through, northern Maine and New Brunswick, was
their homeland, the region of their winter camps. Beginning about
5,000 years ago, they are believed to have made the best and perhaps the
first birch bark canoes. Henri Vaillaincourt thinks so. He is the splenetic
hermit and New Hampshire birch bark canoe maker written of by
John McPhee in *The Survival of the Bark Canoe.* Henri makes the
Maliseet St. John River canoe and the Maliseet St. Lawrence River
canoe—only. The canoe is the finest vehicle ever developed for wilderness travel in the North. The melting of the Laurentide Glacier 12,000
years ago left behind a great deal of water. Maine alone has 5,700 lakes
and ponds connected by hundreds of streams and rivers. In this country
of water and thick forest the wheel would have been of no use. Fortu-
nately Nature provided the materials for something better if man had
the ingenuity to discern their use. Along those many shorelines grew the
white and silver birch to sheath the canoe, cedar for its skeleton, and
spruce, whose roots would lash it all together. This was to be the "wheel"
for Native Americans and for the explorers, trappers, timber cruisers, and
wilderness tourists who followed.

Rivers made Conrad think of history too. Though he was for many
years an ocean-going sailor and ship captain and is known as a writer of
the sea, his greatest, most compelling works, *Heart of Darkness* and *Lord
Jim,* have featured rivers as central characters. *Heart of Darkness* begins
with Marlow and friends aboard a yacht anchored on the Thames mus-
ing on the history of that great river, imagining the many sailors and
explorers, great and small, the famous and failed, who have followed its
course to the ocean and their fate. And of those first "civilized" men, the

Roman legions, who made it their pathway into the interior wilderness of Britain, the savage and unknown land of the Celts. Later, Marlow, speaking for the author, told of his experience on the Congo.

"Going up that river was like traveling back to the earliest beginnings of the world, when vegetation rioted on the earth and the big trees were kings. An empty stream, a great silence, an impenetrable forest."

Umsaskis Lake is still quiet, still uninhabited, still a thoroughfare for passersby in canoes, still a place which conjures the ancient in the imagination. The plane coasted up to the shore at a spot with a small gravelly beach. A canoe was parked at the site. A blonde woman in khaki shirt and shorts and a chocolate Labrador retriever in the bow sat and waited for us. I couldn't wait to get out, load up my gear, tie it down tight, and get going. Jim had some trouble holding the plane to the shore. The first time he got out onto the pontoon to untie my canoe the plane began to blow away from the shore. He had to jump back in the cockpit and redo his approach. He made a frustrated remark. Something to the effect that maybe he shouldn't have tried to do this in this wind. But when he came back in again the wind let up for a moment. The woman, the area ranger, grabbed a line and Jim was able to get my canoe and gear off before the wind puffed up again. In less than five minutes he was gone.

I asked the ranger, Kim, about the wind forecast. She was a cheery sort.

"Gonna blow twenty knots today and tomorrow," she beamed, puffing her chest out, hands on her hips as if she had whipped it up herself and was damn proud of it. I felt sick.

"From the north?" I asked, sure of the answer.

"Yep!" As if to say, "Of course!"

"Boy, I was here last year. I was so lucky. I had a tail wind for three days straight. I nearly made it to Round Pond the first day. Guess this is going to make up for it, eh?" I was thinking something like, if you're agreeable with a bully or a cop or an authority of some kind maybe it'll back off and leave you alone. So maybe this wind would lighten up on me if I spoke of it in this way. As if my acceptance of its authority might placate and gentle it.

"How long you got?" she asked.

"As long as it takes, I guess. I was figuring three days to Allagash Village."

"Ho, it could take you three days to get to the [American Realty Road] bridge!"

I probably looked at her as if she'd just said, "Ho, your entire family was just killed in a fiery crash," but it made no impression.

"Well, you could check in with me at the station but I might not be there when you go by. If not just go on by and check in at the station at Michaud Farm. Good trip." She shoved off in her canoe and splashed away through the waves, her dog catching the spray in its mouth. She had a motor.

I gave no thought to camping there. I loaded my four gallons of fresh water up front, secured together and to the hand hold with a belt. My pack, weighing about fifty pounds, stowed securely within a hopefully watertight dry bag, was strapped in by tightly strung bungee cords in the front third of the boat between the stern seat and the thwart. When I go solo I turn the canoe around and paddle from what is normally the bow seat, facing the middle of the boat, placing me nearer the center line. I clipped a smaller dry bag, the bag containing my cooking materials and the waterproof camera box, to the center thwart. I've decided to store my cooking materials and canned food outside my pack so that I can get at it more easily during the day. Saves me the trouble of dealing with the cords, the heavy bag, all the straps, and the effort of opening all those snaps and zippers to get at my food.

In the smaller dry bag I keep other items I might need quickly or during the course of the day: toilet paper, duct tape, hiking boots with socks, a fly mask, guidebook, rain pants and jacket, and a long-sleeved shirt. I jam my tarp and spare paddle under the heavy bag. Behind me is tied my saw. Around my waist I have my survival pouch with canteen and hatchet attached. My knife is strapped to my lower leg. I've got my hat on, sunglasses, quick-drying nylon paddling pants, nylon T-shirt, fisherman's vest with lots of pockets containing sunblock, bug spray, laminated map, bandanna, whistle, and a Ziploc bag containing trail mix.

I clipped coils of rope to the bow and stern, slopped on suntan lotion, looked around for a moment, and then stopped. Kim was gone around the corner and out of earshot. Jim was over the hills and out of sight. It was incredibly quiet. The water lapped against the shore. An intermittent rustle of breezy branches. There was no other sound. You could strain and still find none. It is one of the things I go for, one of the things I want. At the same time it's mildly unnerving. It means something serious and important. This silence isn't kidding. You are alone. It struck me then, as it has before, the idea of the trip being a ride which once you get on you can't get off. Once you get in there is no going back. There is only going forward. Of course in this case going back wouldn't do you any good anyway, nor would side to side. There is nothing but water and forest. There is point A and point B only. There's no changing your mind or your course. No shortcuts. You can only take what comes. There is no controlling it. You play with what you're dealt, period. Nothing can be added once it begins. But it's no game. It's real. A small slice of it, but real nonetheless. And everything that will happen along the way, good or bad, will be real and can't be changed. There is no quitting or giving up. No substitutions. No disqualifications. There is no deciding it's not fair or you don't like it anymore or you're hurt or tired or hungry or thirsty or too wet or too cold or time's up, once the plane is gone, once you're in. The phrase "you have to" then takes on an awesome sound, no matter how softly it may be whispered in your mind. This is precisely why I go and go alone. And it is why I sometimes dread it.

VIII

AT NOON I PUSHED OUT INTO THE WIND AND WAVES AND FOUND THAT I could do it. On the map the coast line is all smooth lines but down on the water there are irregularities, little indentations, bays, coves, and points of land. Not much, but by hugging the shore real close, sometimes no more than a yard or two off, I could get in behind some land and out of the wind and thus I crept along.

Rounding the points exposed me and I had to paddle hard. Only once did I have to get out as I did at Attean Pond and walk my canoe around, just a hundred yards or so. Otherwise, I quartered into the waves, angling a point off the wind so as to ride over the swells with less chance of splashing and taking in water.

I handled it much better than I had two years before. I think the canoe was trimmed much better this time, more balanced with more weight up front. I also know that I was stronger this time. Because of having been completely overpowered at Attean Pond, and in order to be able to handle that nice-looking, nine-inch-wide paddle I'd bought, I began lifting weights a year and a half ago on a regular basis for the first time since high school. I've kept it up and I want to believe it's done some good.

I was moving along. Within an hour I had seen and photographed up close two moose, one a male with a good start on a nice rack of antlers. They were both chest deep in the lake feeding on the water plants. They saw me coming, twitched and rotated their long ears like radar in my direction. After studying me briefly, chiefly it seemed with their ears more than their eyes, they dunked their heads back underwater and resumed feeding. That's when I paddle hard to close the distance. While they're watching I paddle quiet and easy. I am willing to come up pretty close to a moose in deep water because I think I have the advantage in speed if it's needed.

The wind cooperated and I was able to take my hands off the paddle and onto my camera without getting spun sideways and blown backwards too far. When I was finished I thanked them. It had done me a lot of good to see them and they hadn't run away until I had gotten pictures I'd be happy with. Though it had given me a little distance to make up on the lake from being blown back some, I said out loud to myself, "That's OK. It's what I came for."

I had it in my mind to pass that ranger station and the bridge at the end of the lake as fast as I could. I wanted Kim to be as far wrong as I could make her. I passed it at about 1:30 and didn't stop.

The wind let up in the narrows between Umsaskis and Long Lake along a mile, mile and a half stretch called The Thoroughfare. Here I rode a helpful current and could relax a bit before the eight-mile Long Lake and Harvey Pond ordeal. I saw two more moose along the way but at too great a distance to get a good picture.

I felt the breeze pick up before the horizon broadened and I left The Thoroughfare to enter the next wind challenge. Long Lake deserves its name. It is shaped like a cucumber, about six miles long and a fairly uniform one mile wide. It points due north. I expected trouble here but had gained confidence from my trip across Umsaskis. I was prepared to camp along this lake if necessary and shove off again at evening when winds usually abate or set off at dawn the next day. Until then I intended to inch my way up the west bank, like a mountain climber, clinging to the shore and pulling myself up a bit at a time. I knew that the farther up the lake I went the easier it would get. Waves build a momentum as they are driven across open water so that they are always worst nearest the downwind shore.

I made my way slow and steady hunkered up against the shore as close as I could get. Sometimes the wind threatened to drive me up against the rocks so I had to get deeper. But I always returned as soon as I could, sometimes getting in so shallow that I poled rather than stroked with my paddle. Still, I kept moving forward. If I could cross this lake today, I thought, I'll have the big water behind me and a current beneath me to help me pretty much the rest of the way. I knew the flow of the Allagash to be strong and steady, often pretty fast. The only exceptions are Round Pond which is only a couple miles across and the Musquacook Dead-water, a three-mile section of flatwater about halfway to Allagash Village.

I was making it and felt good. But my right shoulder was starting to hurt in a place I'd had tendinitis a few years before. A cortisone shot cured it then, but the heavy strain seemed to be threatening to bring it back.

A rocky point presented itself to me and I took it as a place to stop and rest. There were nice patches of soft sand amongst the larger rocks. I could set up my little gas stove there and heat up some lunch. Its exposed position allowed for plenty of wind to blow the flies away. I could use the wind as a friend for a little while. It was 2:30.

I pulled over and had a long drink of water, took three ibuprofen for my shoulder and then refilled my canteen. The weather favored dehydration, very windy and very dry. I had no sweat to show for it. My thirst was evidence enough. I sat down in the sand between a couple of shoulder-high rocks and set up my stove. I heated up some Dinty Moore beef stew. Canned food heats up so fast. I have finally learned the value of keeping well fed. I wolfed it down and then sat back for a little while. There isn't much to look at on Long Lake, just water and the even line of the low green ridge which holds it in. There are no mountains on the horizon, no cliffs, or stony formations for variety. Scenery might have been wasted on me at that point anyway. All I can think about when I'm on a windy lake is getting off of it. That was my focus. I was calculating how long it had taken me to get this far and how much longer it would take to finish Long Lake.

I was back in the boat in about a half hour for more of the same. Toward the end of Long Lake grassy meadows appear on the left. I saw a deer and a moose among the cattails. Chemquasabamticook Stream (try saying that five times fast) flows into the lake there and carries with it silt which has, over the centuries, spread far out into the lake. I could see the shallows it created by the tan color of the water. I did not want to get hung up on it. Wading on a silty bottom can be like walking in mud or quicksand. You can lose your sneakers and you can find yourself sinking a lot deeper than you'd like. I had to paddle into the middle of the lake to avoid it. The wind and waves were not so bad. I was nearing the north end of the lake. The wind was less persistent. It huffed and puffed with quiet spells in between. A low engine hum carried to my ears in broken segments on the irregular breeze. Two motor-powered canoes came into view behind me, making their way up the lake. Their bows splashed white spray with a steady beat.

I crossed little mile-long Harvey Pond, the final section of Long Lake, without any trouble and by 5:00 P.M. I had reached the end of the open water and was approaching the former Long Lake Dam. I couldn't see it. But I could hear the water rushing over it. I had been looking forward to that sound. I couldn't wait to get out and stretch my legs, use different muscles, and do some thinking on how to pass over it.

The canoes I had heard on Long Lake slowly passed me. Each carried an adult male, a young boy, and lots of cargo. Square storage containers filled the center space between the seats and rose well above the gunwales. Bags were piled high behind the stern seats. The canoes sat low in the water. I watched them coast past me, their little engines putt-putting them along, as the men lay back against their gear with their legs up, and steered. Their easy comfort irritated me and made me want to beat them to the dam.

The river is rock strewn just above the dam. It was a pleasure to finally do some gentle maneuvering after an afternoon of relentless, hard, and tedious pulling. I wove my way into shore below a high embankment which is a remnant of the old dam. The two long (probably 18 foot) canoes moved sluggishly among the boulders. Their bottoms scraped and caught on rocks that I rode over freely. Their motors couldn't help them there. I reached the landing ten minutes before they did and hopped out with a feeling of cheap satisfaction. I climbed up the bank for a view.

The weather was great, high 70s, hardly a cloud in the perfect blue sky. No haze at all to dull its clarity.

Below lay the rubble that marked the former dam. Rocks and flattened timbers extended from one side to the other, about fifty yards across. When I had been here last year the timbers were barely visible. A good one to two feet of water ran over them. Despite the rocks it had looked definitely runnable, which would have saved me the albeit short portage. But the guidebooks are quite explicit on this point. Don't do it. The wreckage of the dam is littered with protruding spikes which had once served to hold together the massive timbers. Not all are visible. Some are covered by water. Others are camouflaged by streaming green water plants. They are like mines and have torn open the bottoms of even aluminum canoes.

The motor canoes grated against the rocky landing, their heavy bows just poking the shore. The two boys popped into the water and helped pull their boats forward as the men crawled over the baggage toward the bow and stepped onto the dry ground. The boys were all smiles and activity. They ran up the embankment to look at the rushing water below. The men moved stiffly, slowly with tired expressions. They trudged up the hill. Together we surveyed the scene below and discussed the pros and cons of lining versus portaging. They were from central Maine, two fathers in their late 30s with their sons. I guessed their ages to be between 10 and 12 years old. They were in the fifth day of what would be an eighty-mile trip, having put in far to the southwest on Allagash Lake. Even with the aid of their motors they'd had some hard traveling across the lakes to the south: $3^1/4$ miles across Allagash Lake; $7^1/2$ miles across the top of Chamberlain Lake to the Lock Dam portage; twelve miles up Eagle Lake; five more miles along Churchill Lake, with Umsaskis and Long Lake waiting to the north. Days of bad weather, lake winds, rain in the face, wet campsites, and soggy gear. They were looking forward to the end, two or three days off.

We studied the depth and behavior of the water flowing over the rough surface of the ruined dam. Last year I had been tempted by the higher water to run it but had lined my way through instead. This time there was no question about it. I would line it again. The water level was much lower. The worn brown beams looked so smooth beneath the fast-moving slick of water. Some of the iron spikes stuck out a foot above the water which foamed around them as it sped on by. The low water there was the first hint of challenges which would await me further downriver.

I took the bow rope in my right hand and the stern in my left and waded into the river just above the dam. I chose my footing carefully. The bottom was entirely covered with rocks, most of which were slippery with a smear of algae or some other plant growth. By letting out or pulling in on the ropes, it was fairly easy to guide the canoe onto the channel near the broken embankment. The fast flow of the water down over the dam pulled at the canoe and at the ropes in my hands but not too powerfully. I could resist it without great effort. The river did most of the work for me. It carried and pulled my canoe and supplies along. All I had to do was steer and work the brakes. The main thing was to keep my balance. Twenty more feet among the rocks and I was able to step onto a smooth platform of wood, upon which it was easy to slide the canoe and my feet along. The water there was only inches deep, but sufficient to float an unmanned canoe. I let the canoe slide over into deeper slower water as I hopped onto a boulder and guided it out of the flow stepping from rock to rock until I brought the boat to shore. I had saved myself the trouble of all the unpacking, carrying, and packing up again that even a short portage would require. All I had to give in trade was wet feet, a fine deal.

IX

I AM VERY FUSSY ABOUT THE TRIPS I CHOOSE. MY PRIMARY GUIDES ARE the Appalachian Mountain Club's *Maine River Guide* and the DeLorme Maine geographic series of river guides. These books are highly descriptive and very accurate. I look for a river that will give me at least a two-day trip. Something with a distance of at least thirty miles. I want there to be as few lake miles as possible. The entire river section must be described as "wild" in the AMC guide under the "scenery" category. Wild is defined as "Long sections of semiwilderness, with no more than a few isolated camps and occasional road access. Dirt roads may parallel the river within sight or sound but only for short distances, and they do not noticeably alter the semiwilderness atmosphere of the trip. These roads may be closed to the public or altogether impassable."

I don't mind portaging but naturally the less the better. I want rapids but if there are extended Class III rapids or greater, I would need the option of carrying around or scouting it by means of an existing trail. I need a river with water in it. Many of the best rivers or stretches of river run too low to carry a canoe by the end of spring. Water level in June or July then becomes a very chancy thing, depending on the amount of snow that winter in the region, the amount of spring rain and thus the levels of the lakes, ponds, and streams which feed the rivers. Levels can change significantly in just a few days. You can call area rangers, guides, or outfitters and watch the weather but it makes long-term planning difficult. During the spring I can't just pack up and go at a moment's notice. Weather is, of course, an issue in northern Maine in the spring. Snow and ice can extend into May. Being out in a cold dismal May rain has not been fun either. Therefore, I want a river that will still float my canoe at least through June. These are the features I look for. I prefer narrow winding rivers over big broad ones, but that's getting very picky. In short I want a wilderness I can enjoy traveling through on water.

Technically speaking, Maine has no true "wilderness." The route I took is part of what is called the Allagash Wilderness Waterway. The river is rated "wild" in the AMC river guide. Outfitters and guide services describe the region as "wilderness," offering a "wilderness experience." The final 100 miles of the Appalachian Trail in Maine, ending atop Mount Katahdin, is called the "hundred mile wilderness," a legendary stretch which Bill Bryson called "the hardest part of the Appalachian Trail and by a factor I couldn't begin to compute. . . . It is the remotest section of the AT. If something goes wrong in the hundred mile wilderness, you're on your own. You could die of an infected blood blister out there."

Clearly this is not Christopher Robin's One Hundred Acre Wood. Still, it is not quite a "barren and trackless waste," as the dictionary defines "wilderness." It certainly isn't "barren" or a "waste" and there are many "tracks," though few of them will take you anywhere other than deeper into the woods and, as I have said, none is paved. Someone said that wilderness is where there are no people and you don't expect to see any. While there are no homes along the Allagash and the only human residents are the few rangers, you will see other campers and other travelers along the river. Pretty much what an Indian on a hunting trip would have seen a thousand or more years ago or what a timber scout might have seen 150 years ago, before the big lumbering operations and the scattered farms which supported them moved in.

People are on the Allagash all summer long. It has been thoroughly explored and mapped. But since the close of the lumber camps and the long-since-abandoned and reforested farms which fed them, it has been pretty much left alone. "You don't manage wilderness; you manage people," said Tim Caverly, the Waterway's former manager and chief ranger. It is the domain of the plants and animals now, the birds both humble and majestic, the mammals great and small, shimmering fish, and the ubiquitous insect. Humans are only brief visitors and passersby. They are guests, the ones controlled. The place makes you feel that way, like you are not in command, not at all. It is not a feeling you can get just anywhere. The open sea, I'm sure, will give you that feeling. So will wilderness and even near-wilderness.

All day long I had been thinking of just covering the distance, just covering the distance. I'd had my head down concentrating on my strokes. When my head came up my eyes were focused on hitting the wind and waves right or I stared beyond my bow into the distance to where I wanted to be. I have been fighting that attitude on every trip. It is a goal of mine to try as hard as I can to just be where I am; to not be reaching with either my eyes or my mind. I say it to myself. "Be where I am," I say and repeat it like the exercise that it is. I say it out loud for emphasis. There's not much point in keeping it quiet. There's no one to hear me. Nor would I want anyone to. I definitely wouldn't want to sound like some insufferable pseudo-Buddhist. I have been trying to simply focus on the immediate present and on what I am doing and not slip into that unhappy wasteland between the present and the future; between where you want to be but are not and where you are yet ignore and disdain. I say "simply" but it is the furthest thing from simple. Though it is among the great joys of existence, it is among the most fragile and fleeting of conditions. To be fully focused on something in the present, on anything, be it basketball, fly tying, carpentry, music, or paddling, is bliss. It is a state of mind and being which one never forgets and one yearns to return to. People will risk their lives if it is the only way they can attain it. It is why some people repeatedly cling to the sides of mountains or photograph wars. It is the quest for the vivid experience.

The lake crossing was no place for that mentality. I was "reaching" all the way. I couldn't help it and I didn't much want to. But here, finally on the river itself, I could begin to settle in. I was no longer concerned with time and distance.

The main current was so strong it was visible, the water here more active, more striated, and textured. I put myself into it. It was fun to take a good firm stroke and feel myself speed forward. The trees and bushes along the shore slid quickly past me. The smooth water parted cleanly and rushed past either side of the canoe trailing streams of bubbles behind me. I flew over the stones, so clearly visible on the river bottom. The long stringy water grasses, unable to stand up to the rapid flow, lay flat downriver and waved as if in a strong wind. It seemed so quiet here compared to paddling the lakes. There, my ears were constantly filled with the sounds of my own straining. Smells were rich here without the wind to blow them away. Cedar, hemlock, spruce, fir? I don't know my trees as I should. Something evergreen smelled good. A mist began to descend which held the aroma in and gave it a cool liquid essence.

I chose a narrow channel around an island, Cunliffe Island, and as I came around it to rejoin the main flow I encountered a very large female moose. She was planted dead center and up to her knees in water, feeding on the plants beneath the surface. Other than this river being broader and this moose heavier, it was a replica of the encounter I had on Moose River a couple of years before. I got out my camera, set it, flipped off my glasses, turned up the brim of my hat, and zoomed in. All the while I was drifting closer and she was not budging. She stared at me, motionless. She had stopped eating. I have learned what to do next. I broke eye contact and paddled away just as she began to walk slowly toward me. I kept my head down, only watching out of the deepest corner of my eye. She was placated and I was quietly out of reach. But I got my pictures.

There were a couple of campsites nearby. They were cleared and maintained by the Bureau of Parks and Lands. They are patches of cleared flat land with plenty of trees above, a picnic table, and a place to build a fire. Some have outhouses, installed to keep human waste held and concentrated in one area well away from the water. There are no other campsites between these and Round Pond, nine miles downriver.

I felt way too good to stop for the night so I continued toward Round Pond. The air was utterly still. Some black flies and a few deer flies buzzed around me. In patches the river became very shallow. I stood up to get a better look at the best channels to take and poled my way along using my paddle. I have no actual knowledge of poling techniques. I've seen it done a little and read about it. I doubt if my method was correct in any way. But to me, in the absence of witnesses, it was poling.

I knew I would never make Round Pond. It was enough to just be within striking distance of it so that I could cross it during the early morning before the wind rose. I began to look for a spot that could serve as a campsite. It wasn't easy. The forest is thick and for the most part marches right down to the water. Gnarled driftwood, blowdowns, and the beached wreckage of many seasons of storms, floods, and ice-outs line the banks. Relatively clear areas are often marshy. Then there are the impenetrable alders.

I stopped twice to check a couple of spots but had to pass them up. I was getting tired. I looked forward to the night; to being in my bag, in my tent in the cool night; to reading and writing some about the day that had nearly passed. But it's hard to know which spot along the river would be best. Perhaps I'd already passed the best spot I would find. Who knew what lay ahead? I would have been happy to find the spot I camped at last year. It was somewhere around here. It was a level gravel bank, narrow but wide enough with a slightly higher forested bank above it. The lower level where I put my tent and made a fire seemed to have been carved and scoured by the ice which scratches its way downriver in the spring in the yearly tumult called ice-out. The high water which follows wipes the banks clean. But it was early July when I camped last year and grasses, flowers, and weeds had grown knee high up through the sand and rocks on that lower shelf. I cut them down with my paddle. Stones and dry wood lay around everywhere and it was easy to build a fire. A nice breeze kept me bug free and I relaxed and ate my Beefaroni with my back against the upper shelf. The site served well and I have a fine sunset picture of it with my fire in the foreground and my tent in the background. There are a few little wildflowers, a daisy I think and something blue. A large cedar bough frames the top edge of the scene and the river stretches out into the distance, flecked with shimmering orange from the sunset. I couldn't find it. It may have been miles downriver. I may have passed it. The terrain and vegetation can look so different along a riverbank year to year.

I settled on a spot which reminded me of it, a grassy slope at a low angle with the large trees well back from the shore. It was dry and open. But the grass was high and thick and, as it turned out, harbored legions of mosquitoes and black flies. They were glad to see me, happy to have a visitor in this lonely spot. They swarmed to greet me. I still had on my long pants. I cinched the ankles and put on a long-sleeved nylon shirt. The mosquitoes could penetrate it but the flies could not.

I had bought a machete the week before. I was eager to use it on these grasses, weeds, seedlings, obstructing branches, and on anything living or dead which it was capable of slicing or severing. The thing wouldn't work. It did not even cut weeds. My paddle had done better. I discovered the thing had absolutely no edge. I guess you're supposed to take care of that yourself. Meanwhile I was working up a soaking sweat. The sun was sinking across the river. It hovered just above the treetops and bleached my bank with its rays. There was no movement of the air. But plenty of movement in it. I added more bug spray. I rubbed it up behind my ears and up into my hair beneath my hat. A fly mask had sat in the bottom of my small dry bag for two years without ever being used. I had never even tried it on, until then. It made my face pour sweat immediately as I completed the clearing of the campsite. I did a terrible job putting up my tent. First, I put it up inside out. Then I had to reset all the pegs. Same thing with the fly. I was badly disorganized and struggled with every part of setting up camp. The heat, the eye-stinging sweat, and the clouds of flying, crawling, burrowing, bloodthirsty hosts made it impossible for me to fulfill my wish to camp slowly, deliberately, and with love.

My sailor/teacher friend Kevin Rose had once recommended Hemingway's short story *The Big Two-Hearted River,* a story of Nick Adams and a little fishing trip he made alone. It is a simple, beautiful, enormously peaceful story. He camped the way I am trying to learn to camp. He is efficient but unhurried. He finds a soft enjoyment of the routines, his own little sequences, and traditions of camping. He is aware of everything he does. He is, as they say, fully present in each of the moments. He's not rushing to get any of it done in order to get to something else. It is a story I have read to ease the dread, to get my mind right, and it works. Jack London's *To Build a Fire* scares me. Hemingway's story soothes me.

I was Nick Adams' evil twin that evening. I couldn't wait to get the damn tent up, my stuff in it, and done for the night. Speaking of which I couldn't wait for the damn sun to set. I'd have rather camped on the west, the shady bank, but there was nothing there for me. I went down to the canoe and took out my food bag and sat down to prepare a meal but I gave it up. I had lost my appetite. The bugs would have eaten far more than I. No supper that night.

At 8:00 P.M. I was finally in my tent. First, I killed all the mosquitoes and black flies that had come in with me. It was easy. They cling to the mesh, confused, and mostly immobile. I squished them one by one. I took off my shirt and lay down to rest, to let the heat rise out from me, to let my skin dry. My body cooled with the air. The sun was going down.

Sliced rays shone weakly through the black trees across the river. I wet my bandanna with water from my canteen and cleaned and cooled my face. My vest was in the tent with me and in one of its zippered pockets, I remembered, was trail mix. I got some out. Three months before the trip I had bought an Elmore Leonard book. I have read about ten of his stories. I love them, especially for a tired nighttime in the tent. His stories are easy to read, exciting, and short. His books generally do not take up a lot of space. I would never bring a 500-page book on a camping trip nor one which required hard concentration. At the end of the day I'm too weak for it. This one was called *Pronto,* about a bookie on the run. I'd been saving it for this night. In fact I had tossed it directly into my pack as soon as I brought it home. So, with trail mix in one hand and Elmore in the other, I entered the night.

X

EVEN AT HOME IN A NICE BED AND FAMILIAR SURROUNDINGS I NEVER sleep through from one end of the night to the other. In the woods, I don't want to. I want to get out and see the sky. I wake up a lot anyway. If it's clear I'll get out two or three times to look. I live in a very small town. There are still farms in it, three large ones, and a look and feel that people say remind them of Vermont. You could say I live "out in the country." One would expect there to be a minimum of light pollution, little of the haze of mechanized life, and a nice clean clear night sky. But when I see a clear night sky in northern Maine I realize how much my home is within the modern world. Even through the mesh of my tent and the branches of the overhead trees, stars shine more brilliantly than I have ever seen at home. It is a thrill to get out to see them. I go down to the riverbank for a broader view. I can bring home pictures of many of the things I have seen and done during the daytime. But there's no way to bring home the night. It's too bad, because the sky makes me gasp.

I took my flashlight and carefully picked my way down to the river. I had removed most of the deadwood lying around. I'd have removed it all if the bugs hadn't prematurely driven me to my tent. It was only twenty or thirty feet to the rocky riverside. I made it without falling, which was an accomplishment since I kept sneaking looks at the sky instead of watching the ground in front of me. I couldn't wait. I knew it was a fabulous scene. The ultimate beauty in black and white. I stood on the stones and turned slowly around, my neck craned way back. It was cold, too cold I would have thought for mosquitoes, but I began to hear their faint hum. After a little while, 5 or 10 minutes, I returned to my tent ready for another segment of sleep. I had just gotten into my bag and into a comfortable position when a burning itch began on the backs of my hands and then my ankles.

James Davidson and John Rugge, experienced men, wrote an entertaining and informative book called *The Complete Wilderness Paddler.* In it they have a section entitled *The Maddening Sleep of the Undead.* It is about the tiny denizens of the northern forests, the previously saluted mosquitoes and black flies and one other, the most diminutive demon of them all. The Algonquin word for them is *ponk,* which was their word for "living ashes." They are also called midges and no-see-ums. Their bodies are the size of the period at the end of this sentence. Even allowing for their wings it is said they are small enough to slip through even the closest tent mesh. One night, up in Newfoundland, Jim Davidson jumped into the cold river and stayed there for an hour waiting for the unique burning rash-like itch to pass. John McPhee got a dose of them up around Chesuncook Lake in Maine, referring to them as "infernal" and "like an acid, they eat skin."

Thoreau encountered them along the East Branch of the Penobscot.

"They are said to get under your clothes and produce a feverish heat, which I suppose was what I felt that night." As a repellent he employed a "wash" composed of "sweet oil and oil of turpentine, with a little oil of spearmint and camphor." He concluded however, "that the remedy was worse than the disease." I had experienced them last summer on the St. Croix River on the New Brunswick border. But not like this.

The burning spread slow but steady from my hands up both arms to my biceps, from my ankles to my insteps. My skin felt like it was erupting in microscopic bubbles of prickly heat. It began to circle my neck. There was nothing to do but wait it out. Scratching, touching the affected spot in any way, even by the softest rustle of clothing, will only intensify the effect. All you can do is lie there as still as you can and wait for it to pass, which it will, in about 45 minutes. It is a very hard thing to do. The hot itch grows and grows until you wonder what can be its limit. You must turn off your mind to all opposing thoughts, accept it, and relax. You can't get angry. You have to go with it. There is no going against it. I just kept in mind that the longer I could lie still the sooner it would pass. Time was on my side. I didn't even bother to try to distract myself from it. That is futile. Instead I concentrated on it, on its process. I noticed that it came on in waves. I paid attention to its swells and the troughs in between. I rode them slowly up and down. Gradually the waves became lower, weaker, and more widely spaced. I waited it out. What drove Davidson into the river was having it on his face. They've gotten me twice but never, thank God, on the face.

The Maine Indians did not remain in the woods in the summer. Before the flies hit they migrated from their upriver winter camps to the cooler breezy seacoast downriver. They always kept near the water, which was their road system. The St. John, the Penobscot, the St. Croix, the Kennebec, and others took them out of the woods on flotillas of beautiful birch bark canoes to the sea, where they lived easy on fresh- and saltwater fish, scallops, clams, quahogs, lobsters, and crabs. They knew 10,000 years ago that a clam is far easier to hunt down than a deer in a summer forest. Their shell mounds still exist today, some ten to twenty acres across. Their summer fields were there where the corn, beans, and squash were raised which would feed them all year long. They returned upriver in the fall before the first snow, when it was safe and comfortable. They tracked caribou, moose, and deer into the deep snow where their snowshoes gave them the advantage.

When the Europeans came, they too stayed out of the woods. They settled along the coast often in cleared areas abandoned by or taken from the increasingly disease-weakened Indians. The interior of Maine was, and remains, largely unpopulated.

Later, the timber harvest was conducted only in winter. The logs were dragged by teams of horses to a river's edge or onto the rivers and lakes themselves when the ice got thick enough. When spring came and the ice gave way the wood moved with it, downriver to the mills. They did not work in the woods in the summer. It was the forest's smallest creatures which kept everyone out. All but the latest passersby, the tourists.

The rage of the ponkies passed and I fell back to sleep. I awoke a couple of hours later. I could hear the splashing of the river. A good sound to lull me back to sleep. Steady, repetitive, and, it slowly penetrated my dull consciousness, entirely out of place. There should be no watery sound at all here since there were no rips or rapids in this smooth quiet part of the river. Fully awake, I realized there was some sort of large animal splashing about loudly in the river right below my campsite.

"A bear!" I thought, "I bet it's fishing."

I sat up and listened, riveted to the sound, straining for its meaning. Maine is the champion black bear state east of the Mississippi, and Aroostook County, where I was at that moment wide-eyed, is the champion county, by far.

I might have snuck out with my flashlight for a look but, given my intense fear of ponkies, I remained inside. Then the splashing sound moved. It seemed to draw closer. I heard the loud crack of a large dead branch snapping, then another, closer. I could hear the swish sound of movement through the grass and the evergreen boughs as it approached my tent. It seemed to knock over a gallon jug of water I had left next to my dry bag which was not, as guidebooks suggest it should have been, suspended from a tree.

I sat rigid in the tent, all sensation within me channeled to my ears. I could have heard a cough in London. I use a little one-person tent. It is low, about $2^1/2$ feet high at the foot and about $3^1/2$ feet high at the head. It is narrow, with less than two feet of space on either side of me. It is a very light pale green that will pick up any light from the night sky. The creature moved closer, right up to the side of the tent. I could hear its deep rough breathing, the sound appearing to come from a height above my head.

I had three plans, well, two really. The first plan involved weapons and a furious defensive stand, but my only weapons were a dull machete, a $3^1/2$-inch knife, and a puny hatchet, none of which was in my tent, nor, on second thought (which arrived immediately), did I feel quite up to it. Plan One was rapidly discarded. Which left Plans Two and Three.

Plan Two involved the use of my flashlight as a harmless fright device. I would wave it around (turning it on first) inside the tent creating a baffling and disturbing light effect that might send the night visitor hustling back to the river. Plans One and Two also carried the potential for provoking the animal into aggressive action it hadn't intended.

I was left with Plan Three, which was beautiful in its simplicity in that it required of me only that I continue to do absolutely nothing.

The creature then pressed its nose right up against the side of my tent, placing its face about two feet from mine and began to sniff, real loud. It was then that I remembered the trail mix and added Plan 3A, which would feature me pulling my sleeping bag over my head and kicking and screaming with all my might. But only if a big black paw came ripping through the tent fabric.

It sniffed away at my quaking tent for about thirty seconds. That's a long time. Watch it on a clock. Then it crunched and crackled its way back toward the river, where it splashed around for a good hour or so. I was awake to time it. It finally splashed on down the river and into the silence.

It had probably been a moose. The sound of its departing steps suggested a long stride and the sharp sounds of hooves on sticks and rocks rather than soft paws and a shuffling tread. Moose splash in the water too.

It could have been much worse. I might have suffered the fate of two men, twins, camped along the Allagash in the early 1980s. Two brothers just out for a little camping and fishing, minding their own business when, in the dark of night, they were set upon and then carried off—by Aliens. So claims author Ray Fowler in his 1994 book on the shocking incident. He believed that the fact of the fellows being twins was no accident, speculating that the Aliens were probably conducting twin research. Makes sense. With an open mind one can well imagine that an Alien race possessing scientific and technological knowledge vastly superior to our own and enabling them to reach our planet by, among other things, solving the problems of time and space, in their curiosity about the physiology of humans and the phenomenon of twins, after careful planning would go searching for specimens in northern Maine along the Allagash River—WHERE NO ONE LIVES! I'd have been ready though. I had Plan 3A.

XI

I WAS AWAKE AND OUT OF MY TENT AT 4:30 A.M. IT HAD NOT BEEN THE most restful of sleeps. But I rarely feel tired first thing in the morning. The fog was heavy on the river. It had seeped thickly into the bordering forests, wetting every surface and filling the morning with gray. Across the river the black trees could only dimly be seen.

It had been a cold night. I got out of the tent wearing the clothes I had added during the night: my paddling pants, a T-shirt, a long-sleeved heavy nylon shirt, a polar fleece vest, and a polar fleece cowl which covered my head and neck. The temperature was in the 40s. The air was cool and moist on my face. I felt stiff but loosened and warmed up fast. I got my food out of the large dry bag which appeared not to have been molested by the moose. I used a large flat and fairly level riverside boulder for a table and cooked my Beefaroni, which would have been last night's supper, on the little gas stove. I wanted to get on the river as early as possible so I didn't take the time for a campfire. There were no bugs. I sat on a low rock with my knees up high in front of me and ate peacefully in the quiet mist. The gray river slid past silently. The gray air swirled around slowly.

After washing my bowl, spoon, and the empty can, I put away my cooking and meal materials. Packing up took about forty-five minutes.

At home when I am making my plans and preparations and am finally packing, I have a tendency to want to add more stuff, some additional clothing, some sort of new gear. For this trip I discarded my poncho in favor of a light nylon rain jacket and Gore-Tex pants. I bought a new pair of calf-high insulated waterproof socks. I included my polar fleece vest in expectation of cold nights and mornings. Finally I added the aforementioned machete. Everything fits neatly in the backpack and large dry bag, the small dry bag, or the food bag. The canoe carries it all. I'm not on a hiking trip, so why go too light. My list of items is very much like ones recommended by Davidson and Rugge and other wilderness canoe trip guides. It makes me feel like a knowledgeable canoe tripper doing things right. Then I read about people like Henri Vaillaincourt.

> When Henri Vaillaincourt goes off to the Maine woods, he does not make extensive plans. Plans annoy him. He just gets out his pack baskets, tosses in some food and gear, takes a canoe, and goes. He makes (in advance) his own beef jerky, slow-baking for many hours the leanest beef he can find. He takes some oatmeal, some honey, some peanut butter. Not being sure how long he will be gone, he makes only a guess at how much food he may need, although he is going into the Penobscot-Allagash wilderness, north of Moosehead Lake.
>
> John McPhee, *The Survival of the Bark Canoe*

Joe Polis, Thoreau's Penobscot Indian guide on his second trip to Maine in 1853, to the Allagash Lakes and East Branch of the Penobscot, brought the clothes on his back, consisting of a cotton shirt, flannel shirt, flannel underwear, linen pants, wool socks, cowhide boots, and Kossuth hat. He carried a thick jacket, an axe, his gun and ammunition, a blanket, and a large sheath knife. That's it.

Thoreau brought food which included smoked beef, coffee, sugar, tea, plum cake, salt, pepper, and lemons as flavoring for the water. A cotton cloth served as his tent, supported by poles and pegs cut in the woods. India-rubber bags carried his gear which included an extra shirt, extra socks, two waistcoats, six dickies, a thick nightcap, a four-quart tin pail, writing paper, books, compass, pocket spyglass, botany kit, axe, plates, frying pan, jackknife, fish line and hooks, pins, needles, thread, matches, umbrella, towel, soap, India-rubber coat, and a veil as a fly mask. Additional food and materials were provided along the way by the Indian, such as utensils carved from wood; twine fashioned from the bark and roots of trees; medicine, glue, food, and teas from native plants; fish, moose meat, and a dozen products made from birch bark, including writing paper, a candle, plates, bowls and various containers, punk for fire starting, and, of course, material for repairs to his birch bark canoe.

I called Paul last week to ask him if he'd like to come on a canoe trip with me in late July. Just overnight on the St. Croix River. He was enthusiastic, as he is about everything. He liked the dates and the sound of it. But he had to wait and let me know in a week.

"Hey Paul, bring a tent this time, huh."

"Hey Dave, you know if we wanted to be real woodsmen we'd go with nothing but a knife and a loincloth." He draws his inspiration from Tom Brown, the mystic tracker, which means, I guess, that he'll be sleeping under his canoe again and I'll be gauging how much of a wimp I am for bringing all the stuff I bring.

I shed clothing as I packed, so that by the time I shoved off into the slate-colored current I had on what I would be wearing for the rest of the day: T-shirt, fisherman's vest, paddling pants, and neoprene waterproof socks under cold wet sneakers.

It was 6:00 A.M. and wonderfully cool. Nothing moved except the river and me and the mist, rising like slow-motion smoke out of the water. The fog created the kind of cushioned silence like that of an early morning after a heavy snow. The birds sat quiet and drowsy in their nests. No breeze moved the boughs or branches. Only the low rippling sound of my paddle pushing the water and the drip drip when I raised it could be heard.

Visibility was about fifty yards. I could see what I needed to. The sun was a pale white glow through the mist. It had not yet risen above the trees. Vapor coiled slowly off the water in wispy twisting ribbons. Far ahead the air joined the water in a soft seamless wall of gray.

There were many very shallow patches. I had to study the river very carefully to choose the deepest channels. I tried to read the surface for the signs it gives of depth. It will show you if you can understand its language. Competent, experienced canoeists stand up and pole their way along. I can't pole and I don't trust that I won't strike a hidden rock and fall in. I did not want to get soaked while it was still only 50 degrees out. I did alright. I looked for the smooth-flowing surfaces, for the course the water seemed to want to take, for the little tongues and chutes, the dark water. I steered wide of the grassy sandbars, the closely rippled surfaces, the rocks, the waves, and pillows which indicate rocks. I got hung up a few times and had to get out and drag, but never far. Traveling alone in a well-balanced canoe with a slightly rounded bottom carrying less than 300 pounds, I only need about eight inches of water to carry me. Still I began to wonder how conditions would be farther downstream where the river broadens and tends to run even more shallow.

The last time I had been down this river I had checked in, as I must, with the ranger at the Michaud Farm station just above Allagash Falls. I followed him barefoot up to the cabin and sat down in a chair with a back to it, which felt very good. He got out the little square paper that needed to have my name and address put on it along with where I put in, where I'd finish up, how many nights I'd camped and would camp. I had to admit to him that I hadn't used a designated campsite the night before between Long Lake Dam and Round Pond. He didn't say anything about it. The total fee was $10.70. The office was a large square room with nice reddish brown fir walls, floor, ceiling, desk, and chairs. It had a large window facing the river. A huge map of Maine hung on one wall. An equally large map of the Allagash region hung on another. I could have sat there a long time. It was July 3 and I was telling him I was pleased and grateful for the ample water in the river.

"I'm alone so I don't need much," I said. "I guess some years it's too low to even do the trip this time of year."

He had asked me where I thought I would camp that night and we were up at the Allagash map picking a site.

"Yeah, it's holding up pretty good. Had some good rains last week. Helped a bit. Did you call to check?"

I told him I had. He shook his head.

"Had a young married couple two years ago. Came draggin' their canoe down here with what gear they hadn't thrown away." He pointed out the window. "They were out of water, bug bit to hell, bleedin', and worn out. Lookin' like the wrath of God. Been wadin' and draggin' for three days since Round Pond. Beat up terrible. They came this far and said, 'just please get us out of here.' So I radioed for a ride for them and they got took up Allagash Village." He shook his head again. "Happens sometimes. People don't check. They figure, if it's a river it's gonna have water in it."

I was thinking about those people that morning. I was moving along OK though. I can thank my canoe for a lot of that. It is not my original death trap, that veteran of the Seboeis. One month after my return trip with Paul, I drove to the Old Town Canoe Company factory up in Old Town, Maine, to buy, what to me, is the perfect canoe.

I had studied my canoe books for descriptions of design features, dimensions, and materials. I considered the likely uses I would put it to: rivers versus lakes, level of white water difficulty, and associated need for maneuverability. I read canoe magazines and their ratings and recommendations for scores of different brands and models. All the while I was thinking of solo use.

I sent away for the Old Town Canoe Company catalog. I wanted a New England-made canoe. I knew vaguely of the long tradition of canoe making at Old Town, the site of the Penobscot Indian homeland. They continue to own and live on the large Penobscot River islands in that area. The Old Town Penobscots invented the wood and canvas canoe. The company is over 100 years old now, founded in 1898. For hundreds, perhaps thousands of years, Penobscot Indians built their famous birch bark canoes on the same spot where the present-day factory stands. It had been a place where a fine stand of white birch must have grown, was tended, and maintained. It had been a breezy clearing on a hill above the river. A fine place to live and work. They called their canoes *agwiden,* which means "floats lightly." I decided on an Old Town and drove the four and a half hours to the factory store to get one.

I wanted the Penobscot 16. It is 16 feet 2 inches long, weighs fifty-eight pounds and will carry 860 pounds. I wanted the length for its tracking ability, especially important when traveling solo, for its carrying capacity, and for its ability to comfortably accommodate a partner. I did not want a keel nor a completely flat bottom. I wasn't looking for a canoe made for flatwater fishing. I wanted something made for mild to moderate white water use. The Penobscot has what is called a shallow arch bottom which is perfect for my purposes. From the catalog: "Shallow arch bottom canoes have less initial stability but good secondary stability. As the canoe is leaned, it will balance on its side and resist further tipping. Shallow arch canoes work well in waves and white water. Shallow arch bottom canoes offer the best all around performance." It is a narrow canoe, only 34 inches wide, the narrowest canoe Old Town makes over 12 feet. It offers less resistance to the water, which is nice when paddling and doing all the work alone. It is fast.

Perhaps most important, it is made of Royalex, which is a type of tough layered vinyl sandwiched around layers of foam. It is very light, very strong, slides smoothly over rough rocks, will bend and give without losing solidity. It is virtually impenetrable. It is quiet. It is wonderful. Countless times I have bounced off of and slid over and around rocks which, in my old canoe, certainly, and in many others, would have flipped me over directly or hung me up for the river to flip over.

There is a Class III falls on the St. Croix called Little Falls. It is a short series of ledges about seventy feet long at an angle of maybe 30 degrees. It is not difficult. It is a pretty straight run. Still, it is not one you want to go tumbling down. I have run it several times without any problems. I ran it in relatively low water last September. I didn't quite hit the channel properly and ran right onto a large rock. It made a grinding sound as I slowed to a near stop on top of it. In a fiberglass boat of lesser quality it might have torn the bottom open. In an aluminum boat the rock would have grabbed hold and held tight. The powerful flow would have turned me sideways and tossed me over the falls. Then I felt the bottom of the boat press up against my feet and saw it rise, giving with the contour of the rock, and I slid right on over and down the chute, straight as an arrow, and splashed safely into the standing waves beneath. I wanted to hug it or pat it like a good horse.

I had called the factory store before I left home to see if they would have a Penobscot 16. They wouldn't guarantee it. "Things come and go fast. But we usually have some," was the best they could do. When I got there they had three. I took a green one that had been an L. L. Bean demo. My wife said, "Green? How is anyone going to find you if you're hurt and stranded in the green woods somewhere in a green canoe?" It's true. The guidebooks often recommend red. But I like green. It took me all of about ten minutes from the time I walked in the store to the time I had it carried to my truck. It cost me $659, a savings of about $250. I have had it two years now and it has made up for nearly all of my many mistakes.

XII

THE RIVER SEPARATES INTO SEVERAL CHANNELS, LIKE A DELTA, BEFORE IT enters Round Pond. The narrow streams that result flow between low sandy islands covered in high grasses, alders, and scrubby northern hardwoods. It is a busy feeding ground for moose who feast on the abundant vegetation in and around the slow-moving waters. Last year I saw seven moose there within half an hour—males, females, youngsters, and adults. It was raining that morning and I had a good camera with me which I couldn't expose to the elements. So I missed getting their pictures. One reason I came back was for the opportunity to pass through that spot again in the early morning.

I reached the delta before the fog had risen. At the limits of my vision, two moose disappeared into the cloudy shrubbery. A little farther on a black form moved slowly across the shallow channel. The moose took shape as I approached but remained no more than a figure in black behind the thick screen of misty gray, a scene completely without color. It climbed the low bank and stood upon it to watch me. I got my camera out of its waterproof box. It was a strange scene. The murky silhouette was an image without features or texture, just a flat black form in the shape of a moose regarding me as if from underwater. The fog seemed to be the living thing. It swirled and swayed but never thinned or parted. This will make a weird and hopefully cool picture, I thought.

I lifted my camera for the shot and found the lens to be smeared with liquid. I wiped it off and looked through it again. Same effect. I had no lens cap. Condensation had formed inside the box and moisture seemed to have gotten into the lens. Once again I was unable to use the camera passing through the channel to Round Pond. I would have to dry it out before I could use it again. I left the spectral moose in the mist, gazing down at me from above, as I moved out into Round Pond.

The rising sun had room to work upon the wide open space of the large pond. There the fog had lifted high enough in most places to see beneath it to the opposite shore, two miles away. Patches of blue sky colored the air as well as the water beneath. The day was coming to life here. Up ahead white puffy clouds sat on the water like soft airy mountains. Round Pond was the last large open water I would have to cross on this trip and I hoped to do it before the wind awoke. It was still fast asleep. The water was flat and motionless. I moved through it with ease.

There are a couple of campsites on this lower part of the pond. Both were occupied. At the first was a group of men in their 20s, I would guess, with two canoes. At the second was a single canoe and what may have been a mother and young adult daughter. Both groups seemed to be just getting up. Blue smoke from the morning campfire rose over the first camp. People at both were moving about very slowly, limbering up in the cool air. The men spoke softly and very little, the women not at all. They all seemed fully focused on the job of waking up. They seemed surprised to see me. They raised an arm as a wave and stared, perhaps wondering where I'd come from, there being no campsites for ten miles back to near Long Lake Dam, so how did I get up there so fast?

After I passed their camps I came upon a surprise, a tiny cabin or shack in the woods very near the water's edge, tightly enclosed by the forest. Branches of trees brushed against its sides. It was so dark and sat in such deep shade I would not have seen it if there hadn't been a long green canoe in front, its stern end poking out of the woods and into the water. Then a man came down and placed something in it. He was tall and real thin and wore baggy dark green pants, a loose khaki shirt, a broad-brimmed hat with a floppy old brim, and a dark fly mask. He stood up straight and turned his shoulders toward me as I approached.

He waved me over. He had a patch on his upper arm. I presumed he was a ranger, though my map indicated no ranger station for another 17 miles at Michaud Farm. I pulled over. He was the game warden but also seemed to perform ranger duties as well. He asked me if I'd checked in. I told him what Kim at Umsaskis said to me. He said I could check in with him. He seemed to want me to, so I did.

We sat on a rock on the water's edge as he struggled with a blunt pencil to fill out the little square card. Inside his fly mask I could make out a pale face with long red curly hair. The flies were not that bad. I wondered why he wore the mask. I figured, well he's out here all the time and can't be slopping on carcinogenic DEET all day every day, thus the long pants and the mask tucked into the long-sleeved shirt. Just part of the equipment on a calm summer morning in the Maine woods.

I asked if he knew how the water level was downriver.

"Kind of boney. You'll really notice it down past Five Finger Brook."

"Boney?" I'd never heard that term before but I could tell it meant something along the line of "dry as a bone." I was concerned. "Jeez, could be some serious dragging up ahead, huh?" I asked, hoping he would reassure me it wouldn't be true.

"No, you just pick your channels. It should be fine."

It didn't sound fine. He didn't know me. He might presume I was better than I was. The mask that obscured his face had the effect of removing animation and expression from his words. They came out lacking the confidence I would have liked. He was not talkative. He got up to go.

"Might see you down below. Gotta go on down to check some camps." He lifted his hand in farewell and finished loading his canoe. A few minutes later he passed me heading to the outlet of the pond, a small motor powering him along. I got out my map to find the now ominous Five Finger Brook. It was well ahead of me, halfway to Michaud Farm.

The day rapidly brightened. The sky was empty of clouds and held only the faintest trace of a breeze. Some easy playful rapids covered the outlet of the pond as if in reward for completing the crossing. It was fun steering through them. Every mile or so there were other brief rips and

Class I rapids offering cherished variety. There were shallow patches too but nothing I hadn't passed over already further upriver. I rounded a bend and saw the game warden far ahead of me. He was standing and poling his way along. He disappeared around a turn and I didn't see him again. I wondered if he was poling because up there it became especially "boney."

I couldn't stand and pole like him but even from my poor seated angle I was usually able to pick the right water trail, with the help of my canoe. My drags were few, very brief, and far between. Worries of serious trouble sank below my consciousness.

I saw a little fawn feeding along the riverside. The bright morning sun, still shining at a low angle, gave its coat a burnt orange glow. Its comically large ears had picked me up at a good distance but it didn't run. It was a good place to feed and a good place to drink. It was out on its own on a fine morning and perhaps was not inclined to leave it. I paddled soft and slow and then glided on the current. I had left the lid of the camera box open and the camera lens had dried. I took a picture, and then another. The deer looked up at me now and then, curiously, but without wariness. Each time it returned to its activities. I came within thirty feet and might have just pulled up and fed it out of my hand, because the fawn never left. It looked at me calmly without anxiety. Its ears didn't twitch. It regarded me with innocence, as if I were the first of my kind it had ever seen and thus had yet to learn to be afraid. But good enough was good enough and I paddled away talking to it.

The Allagash River is broad with gentle curves and long straight stretches. The scene along the riverside is fairly uniform. It is an unbroken forest. It is deep dark palisades of impenetrable green. You cannot see more than a few feet into the forest at any point. Variety often comes in the form of wreckage: a tree that has fallen down the bank and into the river; the pale victims of past floods or ice rampages lying shattered and stripped of their bark along the riverside, their roots that would not hold splayed out helplessly; a tree blasted black by a lightning strike standing stiff, lifeless, and frozen in its shock. Or it is the sudden presence of movement and life: a heron glides across the river on its sail-like gray-blue wings and lifts up soundlessly to the top of the tallest tree; an eagle perched imperiously above the river ruffles its feathers and then resumes its regal stance; a beaver cuts a **V** into the quiet water or a fawn steps lightly among the alders. I know that at any moment a moose or a bear could step into view. Some claim to have seen cougars and wolves. I go as much for what I might see, as for what I do.

However, on a fifty-three mile canoe trip there will be a lot of tedious paddling, long periods of time, sometimes hours, without the stimulation of rapids, wind, portages, or shallows. There is only the paddling.

I paddle nearly constantly. The only time I stop, other than as a necessity, is for a drink, a handful of trail mix, or to check my maps. I find a comfortable position on my right or left and stroke, stroke. I have a lot of stamina for that sort of activity. I virtually never feel tired during the day while I am active. I will go for a couple of hours or so without realizing I haven't shifted sides. My mind is shut off to the workings of my engine. I think about where I am, where I am going, the weather, the water, the air, what I see and might see, what I might do about this or that circumstance which may arise. I do not think about my actual life. I love my family life and my job and am always thrilled to return to them. But there would be little point in coming out here alone if I brought along a crowd of people in my head. I might think about a song and if I actually knew all the words to a single song, which I don't, I would sing it. I might pass a campsite with someone at it and scrutinize them and their canoes and wave. I wonder what is around the next corner and at times that makes me hurry. But sometimes I think of nothing at all. I challenge my clients when they tell me that, because I want to draw them out or bring them into contact with themselves. Even so, I know that sometimes nothing really is nothing. Freud is alleged to have said that, "sometimes a banana is just a banana." Meanwhile I stroke. My mind drifts and floats. I can be less aware of the work if it is perpetual rather than stopping and starting all the time.

In Tolstoy's *Anna Karenina,* Levin, the rich landowner, has been greatly troubled of late by myriad problems. He joins his peasants in scything a field, seeking an outlet for his frustration and restlessness.

> They mowed one row after another. They moved along long rows and short rows, rows with good grass and with bad grass. Levin lost all consciousness of time and had no idea whatever whether it was late or early. His work was undergoing a change which gave him intense pleasure. There were moments in the middle of his work when he forgot what he was doing, he felt quite at ease, and it was at those moments that his row was almost as even and good as Titus'. But as soon as he began thinking of what he was doing and trying to do better, he became at once conscious of how hard his task was, and his row turned out badly. . . . The longer Levin went on mowing, the oftener he experienced those moments of oblivion when it was not that his arms swung his scythe, but that the scythe itself made his whole body, full of life and conscious of itself, move after it, and as though by magic the work did itself, of its own accord and without a thought being given to it, with the utmost precision and regularity.
>
> Those were the most blessed moments. The work became hard only when one had to put a stop to this unconscious motion and think.
>
> Leo Tolstoy, *Anna Karenina*

On the average I do a little over three miles an hour over the course of a full day, which for me is usually about nine or ten hours in the canoe, twelve hours of total travel time. The farthest I have gone in a day is thirty-five miles. That was done the previous year on this same river. The voyageurs, traveling as many as four to a canoe in canoes as long as thirty-six feet, averaged fifty miles a day. They rose at 2:00 or 3:00 A.M., put in several hours before breakfast and kept on until 9:00 or 10:00 in the evening, or until the northern sun set.

Lewis and Clark sometimes made sixty or seventy miles in a day heading down the Missouri on their return trip from the Pacific. Lewis noted these distances in jubilant italics in his journal.

Joe Polis told Thoreau they could make 100 miles a day descending the St. John River if the wind was behind them.

XIII

I ENTERED THE MUSQUACOOK DEADWATER AT AROUND 9:00 A.M. IT IS A three-mile stretch of flatwater seemingly without current. You have to look beneath the surface at the water plants leaning north for evidence of any movement in the water. The year before I had stopped at a campsite at just about the same hour in the morning, to eat and warm up after paddling for three hours in a steady rain. Musquacook means "birch bark place" in Penobscot. Musquacook Stream enters from the east. It is narrow, squeezed tight by the leaning forest, and looks inviting the way it curves away secretly into the woods.

My original plan for the trip would have had me entering the Allagash at that point by coming down Musquacook Stream. The stream draws its water from a series of very remote lakes to the southeast, principally the Musquacook Lakes. They have been named, unimaginatively, First, Second, Third, Fourth, and Fifth Musquacook Lakes. They vary from small Round Pond–size lakes to larger Long Lake size, each connected by the stream to each other, and feed the stream in its tumbling run to the Allagash. It is twenty five miles from the Fifth Lake to the Allagash River. The total trip distance is the same as Umsaskis to Allagash Village. I loved, though, the idea of this less-traveled path and imagined the cozy forest arching close above me, on either side of that craggy stream.

I had made arrangements for Jim Stang to fly me into Fifth Musquacook, the most distant of the series of lakes, on the Thursday before Memorial Day weekend. You have to hit Musquacook Stream early if you want to ride on water. My only concern had been with some uncertain information regarding some stretches of Class III rapids. Horse Race Rapids are just below the outlet of First Lake and are three-quarters of a mile of Class III rapids described by the AMC river guide as "extremely rough." The guidebook also says there is a portage trail on the left, providing the option of carrying around the rapids or at least scouting them out. However, the maps I have seem to indicate a trail only on the right. Lower Horse Race Rapids, also Class III, appear a little farther downriver. The guide does not say how long they are nor mention any portage trails. It does add the ominous remark that "a loaded canoe may have to be lined in a few places."

None of that struck me as problematic in February, March, or even April. But by mid-May as the looming trip became more real, I began to consider the significance of the unknowns.

The dread was humming hard within me when I called Jim Stang to confirm my flight and to ask him what he knew of the water level. Not too high I hoped. I got the impression he hadn't brought a canoeist in there for a while, perhaps only a few lake fishermen. He wasn't too sure of the conditions of the stream. Just before he hung up, seemingly as an afterthought, he asked, "What kind of skills do you have?"

"What?" I replied. "You mean canoeing skills?"

"Yeah, I hear it can be kinda . . . technical in there. Lotta rocks."

"Well, I'm no big white water canoeist. I can do Class II and short stretches of Class III. But I'd have to see it first. That's why I'm wondering about those trails."

"You should be all right. See you on the 25th," he concluded brightly.

But my light had gone out. "Technical?" "You *should* be all right." Bad thoughts had been placed in my head.

I had called him from work. As soon as I got home I searched my papers and maps for whom I might call to settle some of the questions. The map showed a ranger station right on Second Musquacook Lake.

There is no direct line to the remote stations, so I called the area station in Ashland. The ranger there had never been down that stream and knew nothing of its nature. Several times he tried to put me through to the Musquacook station but got no answer. The ranger, he said, is often out in the field. But he offered to have him call me. Within 24 hours the ranger did call, only to say that he too was unsure and would have someone call me who did know. This exacerbated my nervousness. I could think of no good reason why that stream was so little known other than, for good reasons, few people traveled it. Still, the momentum of months of planning was within me and I felt compelled to try. As much as I feared it, I was searching for ways, means, and justifications to just say, "The hell with it" and go do it. I was having a hard time distinguishing between healthy fear and cowardice.

At the same time I was checking the weather on the Internet. Every day the forecast was different. Different sites had slightly but significantly different predictions. The area was in the midst of a very unsettled weather system. The days were variably described as rainy, partly cloudy with scattered showers, partly cloudy with thunderstorms likely or possible, partly sunny with temperatures in the low 70s during the day, 40s at night. Most sites don't give wind condition predictions. I didn't know what to expect. To some degree that is part of the appeal. Three days before the trip I remained very unsure.

The next day I listened to a message left on my answering machine. It was from a fellow named Joe Mints. I'm not sure if Joe was another ranger or a guide. But he saved me. In a gravelly old Maine twang, which sounded like wisdom itself if not the actual voice of God, his message was, "You want ta know 'bout the Musquacook. Veeery dangerous in theya. Nooo trails t'all. All grown in. You go down theya, you might have a heck of a time gettin' out." Later that same day I made my final check of the weather in northern Maine—heavy rain expected, steady through Thursday, Friday, and Saturday. Highs in the 50s with strong 20- to 25-mile-per-hour north to northwest winds. In short, awful. Not even a close call. I wasn't going. It could have turned out very differently though. If Jim Stang hadn't asked me that simple question just before hanging up. If I hadn't checked the weather one last time. All my imagined disaster scenarios might have come true. All winter long and even into that year's cool rainy spring I had studied my maps and peered closely at the curling thread-like black line that represented Musquacook Stream. I would stare into it and come up with visions of mystery and solitude, adventure and antiquity; a primeval paradise of green trees under blue skies, with always a sharp bend in the stream just ahead and who knows what around the corner. In a moment it was gone and the scene changed to one of blacks and grays and misery and fear. I might well have lost my canoe and supplies in rapids I couldn't handle and couldn't avoid. I might have been stranded in the cold rain in the midst of the solitude I had sought with only the contents of my wet vest and my soaked waist pouch, eight or nine miles across woods and water from the ranger station and fifty miles to the nearest town. I thought of that as I passed the mouth of that peaceful looking stream, and of the *Heart of Darkness,* "The horror, the horror."

There was no horror to be found along the deep slow Musquacook Deadwater, only a lot of steady paddling. My plan was to reach Allagash Falls and camp just a few miles below. It was midmorning and I was already halfway to the falls.

XIV

I passed Five Finger Brook, leaving the Deadwater behind and re-entered the faster flow of the river. The water level dropped immediately but was no worse than it had been above the Deadwater. I continued to study the current very carefully and make frequent decisions on which course to take, usually correct, not always. My feet were constantly wet but not uncomfortably cold. The sun was up and warm. The wind did not rise. A few pesky deer flies and black flies rode with me and tried to take a bite when they could. As long as I kept moving they remained no more than a very minor nuisance.

I continued to see moose, near and far. By the time my trip was done I would see more moose than I cared to count. I stopped on a gravelly beach where the river made a slow wide curve. The beach was on the inside of the bend. The low water level had exposed this clear open shore, which a month or two before would have been under three feet of cold rushing water. I needed to refill my canteen. To do so I had to stop, get out, and go to the bow of the boat where I had stowed and tied together four gallons of bottled water. Well back from the shoreline, behind a screen of chest-high alders, a young moose eyed my approach. If there is anything goofier looking than the full body of a moose, it is the disembodied head of a moose. With its heavy camel nose and kangaroo ears and dopey pop-eyes, it's easy to see why it has made such a good cartoon character. I came in and went about my business as she studied my curious behavior. I sat down on my backpack with my feet on the ground and had a long drink and some trail mix. The moose and I quietly watched each other. When I was done, I pushed off and the moose disappeared into the bushes.

Far up ahead where a point of forested land eased out into the river, I saw some movement, the colors yellow and red, and heard pieces of sound carried on the flickering breeze that might have been voices. As I got a little closer I could see that there were people, a bunch of them, with what seemed to be several canoes. A large, probably guided party at a campsite, I thought. But a lot of them appeared to be waist deep in the water, with a canoe or two. It was hard to identify the meaning of this emerging scene.

The river there is straight, broad, and shallow and I chose a channel which took me away from the group and toward the far side. I counted six men. They were out in the water doing something with a canoe which was half full of water. I thought they might be practicing rescue techniques or the tricky task of getting back into a capsized canoe. I thought I heard someone say something about a "repair" and "duct tape." However, I could not imagine how, on this gentle stretch of river, anyone could possibly have damaged a canoe. They were not behaving in a manner which suggested confusion, agitation, or anxiety. But there was no laughter nor the sound of joking banter one usually hears when a group of guys are together.

I was passing by perhaps 75 yards away. They noticed me but didn't wave or call out to me. They seemed to be serious, but all right. It gave me something to ponder as I continued on down the river.

The current picked up. Ahead I could hear the low roar of rapids as the river tilted downhill. Rocks of all sizes, pale gray where they were dry, glistening black where wet, were strewn in a wide deep arc across the river. Splashes of white hopped all about. I approached quickly. It was easy and fun snaking my way through. Passages were clearly visible with usually a couple of routes available. Sometimes digging in with my broad paddle and holding it hard in place, sometimes paddling three or four hard strokes right or left was all it took to swing my bow this way or that down this chute, past those stones, over that ledge, around that boulder.

In a moment it had passed beneath me and I was cruising among widely spaced rocks on a slower more level stretch of Allagash which alternates regularly between fast and slow.

At the distant end of a long straight length of river, something bright red seemed to be sitting in the water. It was not a canoe. I squinted hard through my sunglasses. In a world of natural greens and blues, bright red clearly did not belong. There were no flora or fauna which fit that scene. I become hungry for a curiosity of any kind as I paddle the long lonely lengths of the broad Allagash. An unidentified red thing more than qualified.

I had to get very close before I could even guess what it might be. It was definitely man-made. Perhaps a container of some kind. It was perched upon a flat dry rock. A gas can. A red plastic five-gallon gasoline can sitting upright and looking bright shiny new. There was something else in the water farther down. An aluminum insulated cooler also resting above the water on an exposed rock like it had been placed there. I stopped myself against the upriver side of the boulder, opened the cooler, and looked inside. It was packed with food, cold cuts, mayonnaise, cheese. It looked pretty fresh. I had hoped to find a Coke. Fifty yards farther, a soaked swollen rolled up sleeping bag. A new paddle with the red store sticker still on the flat of the blade and a tube of suntan lotion shared another dry stone nearby. Somebody must have capsized, probably in the rapids I had just passed through. Whoever it was hadn't bothered to tie down any of their gear. But where were they?

Now this was a mystery. Who were these people and where had they gone? I wondered if the debris was somehow linked to the party of men upriver. I thought of returning to them. But the idea of plowing upriver against the current and through those rapids, alone and without a pole or poling skills, quickly dissuaded me. If canoeing etiquette demanded otherwise, I would have to plead ignorance.

The year before I had been startled by the appearance of twin log cabins facing the water atop an eroding riverbank. They had been worn gray and abandoned long ago. In each cabin, two small square windows were cut into the thick pine logs and sat like empty black eyes on either side of oversized doors. The doors hung upon huge rusted hinges and must have been a very bright green at one time, for a faded vestige of it remained. Its chimneys were bent and crumbled a bit at the top from too long exposure to too many winters' terrible winds and the freezing and thawing of too many storms. All in all the cabins looked quite sturdy, still with their roofs unbowed and their firm heavy walls standing straight and strong.

Aside from the ranger and game warden cabins, they were the only man-made dwellings to be seen between Umsaskis Lake and Allagash Village. They stood in a small clearing which even now had not yet been entirely retaken by the forest. It is called Cunliffe Depot. It was a logging camp long ago in the days before the trucks entered the woods. Evelyn McBraierty, who held my truck for me at Allagash Village, asked me if I had seen it. "I went to cook there once when I was a young girl. Back then all the men went into the woods and all the women cooked." I don't know her age. She may have been sixty-five, seventy, or eighty. I had the feeling though that she spoke of a far distant time. She smiled with the fond memory of the long ago adventure, that rite of passage. Her father and uncles, brothers and cousins had all worked in the woods. Or they had hauled supplies up to the camps by horse boat—teams of horses hitched to flat boats that dragged loads upriver through the water and along the shore when there was one. Or they raised horses for the job of dragging cut timber from the woods to the river. Or they grew hay to feed them or crops and beef to feed the men. Everything was the lumber business. And the business seemed like it could not ever end, that there could never be enough saws and men and horses or time to ever equal the vastness of a forest which even then held secret distant places that no man had ever seen.

I did not stop that first time because I was caught up in hurrying, in covering distance. I did not stop this time because of the flies. If I pass this way again, I will try harder.

I was nearly to Michaud Farm ranger station. Michaud station had once been one of a network of farms strung out along the Allagash and the other logging routes. Some had been established by pioneers and families who sought a degree of solitude which only Maine and the Far West could provide. Most were cleared by men who saw it as a good, albeit hard, business in support of the booming logging industry which consumed as much as a farmer could grow and paid a fine price for it too, given the intense demand and the slight competition. Practically speaking, supplies could not be brought up from farms to the south. The absence of roads and unreliability of the rivers necessitated food and fodder sources upriver in the woods near the camps, thus Michaud Farm.

I was thrilled to see the large cabin and wide grassy lawn of the ranger station as I rounded a wide bend in the river. I was looking forward to getting out of the canoe and walking around. In particular, I wanted to talk some with the ranger. I wanted to ask him what it was like to spend the winter there. I wanted to ask what ice-out sounded like. Did he believe there were cougars and wolves in the woods? There are reports of sightings, some from reliable outdoorsmen, but no conclusive physical evidence of a native population. I wanted to ask him to tell a tale or two; canoe disaster stories or funny moose and bear encounters. And I wanted to tell him about the mysterious debris in the river.

Shallow rapids crossed the river on the approach to the station. I picked the wrong channel and ran aground. I had to get out and drag back upriver a bit so I could get into the right one. Two women stood watching on the lawn. One wore what looked like a ranger uniform. They moved their hands in front of their faces in that slow steady waving motion which means black flies. They approached as I came to shore. The flies surrounded me as soon as I got out of the canoe and I joined them in their hand waving.

The uniformed woman, a stocky blonde in her 30s, was the receptionist. She came forward.

"Checking in?" she asked with a smile.

"Well, I checked in with the game warden on Round Pond." I showed her the card.

"Where did you put in?"

"I was flown in to Umsaskis yesterday."

The receptionist turned to the other woman who was drawn forward by her look. She wore a worried smile.

"She's looking for her husband and her brother with their two kids," the receptionist told me. I had passed two men in two heavily laden canoes with two young boys way back at Long Lake Dam.

"Two boys?" I asked.

"Yes," the woman said coming closer. I described the four I had seen. They seemed to be the ones. They were from central Maine and had put in far to the southwest on Allagash Lake on an eighty-mile trip. They were overdue.

"Probably held up by the winds on the big lakes," I told her. But, I thought to myself, they had engines on their boats. An image entered my mind of their canoes, carrying two persons each and supplies stacked high between them and the weight and the shallow water where motors were of no use and black flies in calm air and the frightful story of the bedraggled couple the ranger at that station had told me. But I kept all that to myself.

She had been waiting for them all day. I had spoken to them briefly and had been so impressed by the cheerful attitudes of the two 10- to 12-year-old boys after five days on the water and away from all the comforts and electronic pastimes of the modern American kid. Their fathers did not appear to be holding up quite so well.

I told her they seemed fine but were certainly well behind me and may be slowed further by the shallow water.

"But they spoke of you constantly," I joked. Her worried smile had returned and she waved her hand about her face as she looked back upriver.

There was no point in hanging around. The bugs were bad and the ranger wasn't there to speak with. The receptionist was not a ranger. She was new and apparently not experienced or knowledgeable. I forgot to tell her about the debris. Not too long ago all one needed was a high school education to be a Maine ranger and the hiring was non-competitive. Jobs did not have to be posted. If there was an opening, it was simply filled, with little training to go along with it. Now most successful candidates far exceed the minimum qualifications (a two-year degree in forestry or related field), typically holding multiple two-year, four-year, and graduate-level degrees in areas such as forestry, biology, computer science, education, wildlife management, and criminal investigation. Applications come in from all over the country, drawn by the appeal of one of the last large wilderness areas in the country.

Besides needing to have an educational background that is competitive, applicants must pass a written test measuring their knowledge of the fire service, problem-solving, and communication skills. They must complete a physical aptitude test which includes, among other things, running a mile and a half in less than 11 minutes 40 seconds. Those who survive this must face the oral board review in which decision-making skills, character, confidence, and initiative are challenged and judged. One in fifty is hired. Those lucky few receive ten weeks' training at the Maine Criminal Justice Academy, followed by yet another ten weeks of specific forest-ranger training. Rangers are often the only law in the North Woods and are often confronting armed men, hunters, and those breaking hunting laws.

Most ranger candidates bring experience and expertise to the job derived from having been woodsmen, foresters, surveyors, police officers, and people used to being outdoors perhaps all their lives, and thus have within them an education both deep and broad. If someone in the Maine woods runs into trouble it will be a ranger he must rely on. There is no one else. A canoeist incapacitated along a lake or river must be taken by his partner, by canoe, by water to the nearest ranger station for help, first aid, and evacuation if nescessary. If traveling alone or without a working canoe, a person in trouble waits until someone comes by who can provide transportation or go on ahead himself and inform the nearest ranger. Unless you have a thousand dollar satellite-link phone, you cannot call for help. There is only the ranger. I had wanted to talk to a person like that.

XV

BEYOND THE STATION THE RIVER BEGAN TO FILL WITH ISLANDS WHERE sand and gravel had piled up over the years, held together by the roots of trees and plants and grasses whose seeds had blown in or washed up on their rocky barren surfaces and taken hold. Silver maples grew on the larger islands, leafy trees which can't compete with the evergreens on the shore but flourish on the river islands. The islands were of all sizes. Some only a few feet across, others were the size of tennis and basketball courts. A few had grown to the size of football fields. They change every year, growing or shrinking, appearing and disappearing, cut, sculpted, ravaged, and renewed by their creator, the water, which is always at work around them.

I picked my way through the channels which curved between them. It was late in the day for moose. I saw none. Like the entry to Round Pond, the area must be a favorite spot for their morning and evening meals.

When I cleared the islands I could hear the falls, the magnificent forty-foot Allagash Falls. Reaching them had been my goal for day two. It was 1:30 P.M. on day two and I could hear them. I was only fourteen miles from Allagash Village. I could be there by nightfall if I felt like it. The worries I had been nursing for weeks, drawing their nourishment from bad experiences and bad thoughts, from the dread possibilities of all that could go wrong, roused by the breezy branches on the road to Millinocket and the white-capped waves of Umsaskis, stirred by low water and low-water stories of boney riverbeds and the random appearance of the unexpected and unexplained, now could find no voice within me, drowned out as they were by the jubilant applause of Allagash Falls.

The year before a strong tail wind had blown the roar away from me so that I could hear nothing of it as I approached. This time the wind was slight and the noise tremendous, one of the great sounds of nature.

I coasted up to the clearing below the portage trail and began unloading my gear for the one-third of a mile carry. I had been picking at trail mix all along the way but hadn't really eaten much of anything since breakfast at 5:00 A.M. Still, I hadn't felt hungry. But when I landed and found myself in a covering breeze and not pestered by flies, I found that I was starved. I got out my little stove, set it on a wide rock and heated up some beef stew. I sat and ate it in the warm sun, sitting back against a warm rock, surrounded by the sound of water on a clear blue day.

It took three trips to get all my stuff over the low hill around the falls, $1^2/3$ miles altogether. It is a good trail. Who knows how old. White men rarely improved upon Indian trails or sought to. Maliseets, and probably others, speared salmon there since before history began. They carried their canoes around too, because they weren't fools and didn't treat deadly white water like a carnival ride. So the trail is old and good. It is mostly dry. It has been well maintained and is not obstructed by intruding branches or blowdowns. There are many rock surfaces worn porcelain smooth by thousands of passing moccasins and shoes and the soft stroking of falling rain and melting snow.

There is also a heavy iron ring drilled deep into the rock along the path at a point just above the brink of the falls. It signifies the time when Man brought violence to the falls in the form of the log drives. And he brought brand new sounds. For 10,000 years nothing was greater than the sound of water falling onto rocks, steady, relentless, solitary. Until the log drives came with the big new sounds. They were the rough sounds of men who had not come laughing to hunt or fish and who were not silent travelers in birch canoes. The sounds of working horses and iron wheels and chains, chugging machines and whining cables, of great straining cracking groaning jams of timber piling higher and higher at the narrowed channel of the falls, and the sound of dynamite and chaos and the colossal crashing noise of the jam break burying the water and even the ancient sound of the water itself.

The lumberjacks were the cowboys of the North Woods and lived a life and worked a job at least as hard and dangerous. They left their mark on the landscape and their names along the river: Harvey Pond where John Harvey cleared the land in 1884 for Harvey Farm, now long gone; Cunliffe Island and Cunliffe Depot (Cunliffes were the first white settlers on the land Evelyn Pelletier McBraierty now lives on at the junction of the Allagash and St. John Rivers); Turk's Island where a horse by that name had drowned, tied like a slave to a horse boat; Michaud Farm, cleared just after the Civil War; Ghost Bar Landing, where a white pine crushed a man who was cutting it (the huge tree had been left on the bank where passersby claim to have seen the ghost of the slain lumberjack pleading to have the log put in the river so that his soul could find rest); and McGargle Rocks, a few miles downriver from the falls where a log driver by that name was killed while trying to pick (loosen) a jam.

Clearing a jam was among the most dangerous jobs any human being has ever freely engaged in. And it was a routine part of the business. Men were sent out onto the pile with their peavey poles to try and find the key logs which held it together. This involved a lot of pulling and poking around, like trying to figure out where to start in untying a complex knot. If the jam gave way before the men could clamber off it, death was virtually certain. That is what happened to McGargle. But lumberjacks were nimble fellows with a fine feel for the wood and the water. "Foam walkers" they were called. They expected to be able to sense the tell-tale shifts and simply run off the jam if they needed to and nearly always did. If a likely log was identified, a rope was tied on, the men got off, and men and horses on shore would give the rope a good pull.

In cases where a jam was inaccessible (as, for instance, within a deep chasm) or too dangerous even for lumberjacks to be ordered onto, such as at the brink of a high falls, more elegant methods were called for. For example, a man might be suspended above the jam by a rope and either dangled above it or set down lightly upon it to pick and pull with his pike-like peavey. The rope ran through a pulley on a tall pole that leaned out over the river at a 45-degree angle. Raising or lowering the pole and the rope allowed men on the bank to guide the placement of the man on the jam, and to pull him off if it suddenly gave way. Any volunteers? When all else failed there was dynamite. But dynamite damaged some of the wood. Cheaper to risk the men. The narrow channel and rough rocks of the falls were a chronic confounding impediment to the log drivers, a place of notorious mountainous snags. No doubt they cursed it and sometimes blasted it. But there are other stories to be told here.

Later, sitting on Evelyn McBraierty's front porch waiting for my truck to be delivered, I heard another story. A relative had come by to visit, one of several who passed by or stopped in during the couple of hours that I waited. Evelyn is a Pelletier and the Pelletiers are one of the oldest, most numerous, and prominent of Allagash Village families. The relations were varied and hard to figure out: a grandnephew; an in-law of some sort; a niece whom she had raised as her own, with her own two children; and the two men who were their fathers. They all seemed to be struggling with troubles and sad stories. I suppose Evelyn had her own. I wasn't quite sure who the woman was who joined us. We weren't introduced. Just " 'lo there" and she sat down. She too had seen hard living and looked it. She might have been 25 or 35. Dark, and tired looking under the eyes with old teeth and brown unbrushed short-cropped hair. She had a son at home on house arrest wearing the bracelet which made his whereabouts known 24/7 to probation and the police. She felt lucky to have gotten a night shift job recently at a factory doing assembly work up around Fort Kent or Madawaska, I think. It might have been Presque Isle, the big town up there.

Evelyn said to her, "You remember that story 'bout that canoe went over the falls, oh, must have been 1990 or 1991? Young girl went over and got killed and her husband standin' on the shore with two life jackets in his hands. 'Twas their honeymoon." She was prodding the younger woman for help with the memory of it but got no reaction but a dull shake of her head. It didn't ring a bell with her. But Evelyn continued.

"Well the fellow, the husband, was just standing on the rocks at the top, all wet and saying how he'd got out but she went over. But the people said, she'd gone over in the boat so why didn't he too? He said he was in the back of the boat and when he saw the falls ahead he jumped out and thought she did to. It took about a week to find her body down under the rocks and people said she had these bruises all around her neck, and him with those two life jackets in his hands," she concluded, with what seemed to her to be the clincher.

"What? Like she'd been strangled or something?" I asked. She nodded her head slowly up and down.

"Couldn't prove it though," she said, as if it were just another case of bad luck and hard times and the wicked getting away with it and she'd seen plenty of that.

XVI

I PULLED OUT INTO THE FAST-MOVING WATER BELOW THE FALLS AND
rounded the big turn to the left which put the falls out of sight. The
river grew quiet again. It was only 3:00 P.M. but I had made up my mind
long before to camp at one of the Big Brook campsites three or four
miles downriver from the Falls, even if that meant stopping for the day at
4:00 P.M. That is early for me. I usually like to keep moving until evening
and be in bed a couple of hours after finding a campsite.

The year before I had made the mistake of pushing on. I had
reached the falls at about the same time on day two of the trip. After the
portage I headed for the Twin Brook campsites eight miles downriver,
which would have left me a wonderfully easy six-mile trip the following
morning. I love to finish a trip that way; to get up early, catch the best
part of the day on the river, and have the rest of the day feeling fresh and
full of energy for the long drive home. The problem was, I missed both
Twin Brook campsites. One was on the west bank high above the water
and while I do remember seeing a spot which looked like it might have
been cleared for camping, it was too high above me to get a decent look
and I could find no sign. All the campsites along the Allagash are marked
by small but clearly visible square brown signs, bearing the triangle tent
symbol and the name of the site in bright white print. I kept going, figuring, why guess? When I get to the campsites I'll know it. Meanwhile I

was passing them both. A low island sits in the river between the camps, dividing the river in two. I took the west channel and as I passed unknowingly beneath the West Twin Brook camp, the East Twin Brook campsite slid behind me on my right, hidden from view by the island. The sky was gathering clouds and as they grew and their undersides darkened I studied the shorelines for anything that might do for a camp. It was about 5:00 P.M. I got out and tried a couple of spots but found them too rocky to drive a tent peg into.

Then the sky began to clear. The sun shone bright and low from the west, glancing off the water against the side of my face. I was hot and tired. Suddenly, a house! Then a few more. A car sped by glinting in the sun between the widely spaced houses, moving quickly and smoothly on what had to be a paved road. What the hell is this, I thought. Then, straight ahead, a few hundred yards away, a road, with guardrails and telephone poles and street lights, crossed directly in front of me. I got out my map and sure enough, I had entered Allagash Village. Five thirty in the freakin' afternoon on only the second day of a three- or four-day trip and I was in God damn civilization!

I was mad. No way did I intend to spend only one night in the woods after having gone to all that trouble and come all that way. Besides, where would I sleep? In a motel? I was certainly in no condition to drive nine hours home. I was dead tired and my back was killing me. I'd been twelve hours and thirty five miles that day and had reached my limit. I scoured the riverbank for anywhere to camp, finally taking a spot literally right around the bend from the takeout place, below the Route 161 bridge. But it was clear, level, and out of sight from any house, so I took it and went to sleep on four ibuprofen (greatest stuff in the world) and no supper.

This time I would not put myself in that position. I pulled in beneath the high bank of North Big Brook camp and hauled my stuff up the steep fifteen-foot embankment to a beautiful flat clearing with a picnic table under tall fragrant spruce and hemlock. Compared to my last camp this was like a spacious plaza. There was even an outhouse and stone campfire site with a heavy metal grill. It was almost too nice. It seems like cheating to go into the "wilderness" and have places like this available. They are among the reasons why I allow myself to get into situations where I am forced to rough it in a campsite of my own making. I understand the reason these sites exist and can't argue with them. They keep human activity, our waste, fires, and general destructiveness contained within prepared areas.

That afternoon I was grateful for it and the ease of camping it allowed. Flies and mosquitoes were present but not the torment they had been the night before. A gentle breeze puffed through the trees. I put on dry socks and my hiking boots. They felt luxurious after a day of wet feet in damp sandy old sneakers. The simple sensation of standing, being upright, unfurled from my paddling crouch, walking on soft smooth dry ground on soft firm dry soles was like a salve to my tired parts. I put on a long-sleeved shirt against the flies and looked for a tent site. I chose one down a short path among some low hemlocks and away from the central clearing. Others could conceivably stop here and if so I wanted to be well away from them when I went to sleep. Insects buzzed around me while I set up. But it was cool in the shade and I took my time. The spot needed no clearing. I brushed away a few sticks and pine cones and lay down my ground cover, a 4 x 8-foot piece of tarp I'd cut from an old pool cover. I lay down on it, getting a feel for how level and smooth it was, feeling with my back for roots and rocks. I lay the tent down and pushed pegs through the loops into the soil. They slid in easily all around. The arched poles raised it into the form and space of a tent. I put the fly on too, though the sky was clear. Things can change and I never want to get stuck doing it in the rain in the dark. I reset a few pegs, pulling the whole thing nice and taut.

I laid out my air mattress and pumped it up until it was soft and spongy, not too hard, especially in the pillow. I dumped my backpack out of the dry bag, opened it up, took out the bag of clothes and the sleeping bag, both double bagged in heavy three-mil trash compactor plastic bags. I brought the clothes, the sleeping bag, and the inflated air mattress around to the tent opening, unzipped it, and shoved it all in, mattress first, as fast as I could and rezipped it, hoping to let in a minimum of the little vampires. The ones that had snuck in I would execute later.

I hung my vest, survival belt, and knife from a nearby tree.

My maps and a guidebook were on the picnic table. I sat down and looked them over rechecking my location and the distances ahead. I knew where I was and how far I had to go. And the news was good. So good it deserved another look.

It was probably 5:00 and I had a lot of time to kill. I wrote some in my journal. I am never able to write much at camp or along the way. I love the idea of it. I can picture easy scenes of contemplation and creation, back against a tree, hat pushed up, pen in my mouth, and pages opened across my raised knees. But I can't do it. I can't slip easily into that mode. Go from the thoroughly physical to the placidly cerebral. The tight to the broad focus. The fine motor task of writing is grueling after the large muscle work of the day. I cannot make the transition to the reflective mode or whatever it is which allows me to write. It is too soon for me. Instead I make notations and brief references to times, places, and events.

- up at 4:30 A.M.
- out at 6:00 A.M.
- Allagash Falls 1:30 P.M. Dinty Moore
- plenty of moose
- great conditions and weather
- low water—several draggings
- someone lost their gear—strewn all over the river
- a friendly deer
- Michaud Farm station—wife looking for the four I'd seen at Long Lake Dam
- my concern about the heavily loaded canoes in those waters
- bugs
- camp at North Big Brook

They are memory anchors. Markers for larger ideas and experiences. I expand on them when I get home.

I went for a walk. Trails left the camp heading north and south through the woods along the riverside. The one out of camp to the south probably led to the South Big Brook campsite. The trails were narrow, pine needle brown paths, edged with puffy mosses and low pure white flowers centered upon a base of green leaves. They wound through columns of rough-barked evergreens into the still, dark green woods. Home of the mosquito and the fly. I went down both trails a ways but retreated each time to the more open air of the camp.

I didn't feel particularly hungry but I gathered wood to make a fire and cook some Beefaroni. It would give me something to do and generate some smoke which would help with the flies. Fires keep you company. They are active, interactive if you wish. I included some mossy branches and green wood to increase the volume of smoke. I had finished my meal and was burning up the paper towels I had used to clean my bowl, pot, and spoon, when below on the river, three canoes appeared. I stood above them on the height of the riverbank and waved. They waved and kept on around the curve of the river. They were moving real slow, near the shore, and seemed to be looking to camp. Headed for South Big Brook camp. Then they came back. They called up to me.

"Mind if we share your camp? The next one's all filled up."

"Sure. Plenty of room here. I'm alone." I go to a real campsite and sure enough I end up with company. I strenuously avoid this eventuality. I never seek it out. I presume it will feel like an intrusion and a distraction. I imagine I will not like it and prefer to be alone and I plan accordingly. But when I come face-to-face with people along the way I am always glad I have. A connection is formed naturally and immediately. We have a passionate common interest which has brought us hundreds of miles and days of hard traveling through shared risks and experiences, to the same place at the same point in time. We know something large and important about each other before we even speak. We can talk about it. We want to talk about it and to listen, something which is rare and fleeting with most of the people at home, though I know them so much better.

Last year I met four guys my age on the portage around Allagash Falls, three men from Massachusetts along with a Maine guide. They admired my canoe, which I then had a chance to talk about, in detail. The town I live in is small and obscure with a population of 2,500. One of the guys had once worked at a large farm which is there. My son had worked there the previous summer. We knew some of the same people. They offered me Chips Ahoy chocolate chip cookies. I turned them down at first, but when they asked again and I saw that they had bags of them and they encouraged me by saying they only had one night left on the river and couldn't eat them all, I took three packages and enjoyed them as much as anything I have ever eaten. It's not much of a story. I met some guys who gave me cookies. The circumstances are everything.

The morning of my third day on the Moose River trip, I walked into the camp of two men with their young sons, along the portage around Attean Falls. I had missed supper the night before because of rain and the need to quickly camp, set up my tent, and jump in. I skipped breakfast that morning in a hurry to finish up the trip and believing trail mix would suffice. The morning was cool, foggy, and damp and I soon felt chilly and tired. I trudged drearily up the wet path through the dripping trees and gray wet air right into their campsite, which straddled the path. The men were up and had a good fire going beneath the cooking pot. Smoke rose around it and blended into the mist in the overhead boughs. Hammocks were slung between trees beneath tarps. Two were empty. Three held sleeping loads, the three young sons.

I felt I had barged into someone's open-air home. I said "Hello" softly, trying not to startle the sleeping or the awake. The men greeted me without hesitation, as if I was an expected relative a little late for the cookout. They wondered where I had come from though, it being the crack of dawn and seven swampy miles from the nearest established campsite.

They had finished preparing some ramen and offered me some. The cook more than offered. He just started pouring some into a can for me. I couldn't say I had already eaten and didn't want to. I drank it down and chewed the hot noodles, feeling the warmth spread throughout my body like a fine drug, energizing and exhilarating.

They were retired career Army veterans, who did home remodeling. Finding that I was a psychologist who worked a lot with teenagers, the guy who served me the ramen opened up a long lament about his trials and tribulations coping with a hellacious teenage stepdaughter. If I'd had a card on me he'd have greedily taken it.

After I had eaten the noodles and drank the broth, we walked down to the falls. Attean Falls are hardly that. They are a mild gradual slope, filled with rocks. In high water it's a good Class III ride. But in August, at low water, it was a wide rock garden, wetted by pools and slim streams and too shallow to paddle through.

The boys had roused themselves and joined us in climbing over the jumble of rocks at the water's edge, looking for the best route for me to line my canoe. I saw the five of them for the last time as they stood and watched me wade by, my ropes in hand.

XVII

THE SIX MEN FROM THE THREE CANOES PULLED THEMSELVES, GRUNTING, up the nearly vertical path to the campsite. Exposed rocks and tree roots served as a rude stairway. They ranged in age from about 25 to 50 and in size from fat to fit with a slight edge going to the beer bellies.

Camping in these environs is a great leveler. Visible differences in class, income, and education disappear. There are no fancy campers here. Everyone looks like a bum.

They began unloading their gear immediately and it was a formidable horde. I helped them haul cooler after heavy cooler up the cliff-like embankment.

After setting up their tents they opened their coolers and began piling food and its accessories onto the long table until the top and both benches were filled. Then they began to cook. I walked around incredulous at their bounty and the rough harmony of their routine. Each cooler was a cornucopia. They had hot dogs, sausage, ground beef, cheeses, mushrooms, tomatoes, onions, peppers, various cooking oils, breads, potatoes, three kinds of rice, salt, pepper, Tabasco, ketchup, mustard, olives, pickles, teriyaki and Worcestershire sauces, spices, crackers, more cheese, bags full of shelled peanuts, a hunk of solid beef about $2^1/_2$ feet long and at least 4 inches thick. They had to chop out steaks with a hatchet. They had orange juice, wine, whiskey, and countless beers. I haven't included their breakfast or lunch food, the stuff I didn't see, or the stuff I have forgotten. On the other hand, they had *no water*. I gave them a gallon.

They got four fires going; a big fireplace blaze and three gas stoves set up on the table. The youngest of the bunch and the most garrulous, a round, red-faced little guy with a lot of huffing puffing energy and red curly hair under a Boston Bruins baseball hat, hacked away at the slab of beef and threw seven Flintstone-size steaks on the grill. I looked at the grease and blood smeared on the table and dripping between the planks into a puddle on the ground and thought of the bear/moose visitor I'd had the night before. But I wasn't about to criticize.

They were all from the building trades, laborers, electricians, steel-workers, and carpenters, who had all worked together at one time or another on the Big Dig in Boston. They did a trip of some sort every year together, mostly hiking and camping trips in the White Mountains of New Hampshire. This was their first long canoe trip together. They had driven all the way up to St. Francis, Maine, on the St. John River between Allagash Village and Fort Kent, then been taken three more hours on dirt roads by the noted old guide Norman L'Italien, to a put-in at the logging road bridge just above Round Pond. After that very long day of driving, they had camped at Round Pond, crossed against the wind the day before (while I was crossing Umsaskis), camped just beyond Musquacook last night, and made it another ten miles today. These guys believed in long meals, slow starts, early finishes, and enjoying themselves. They also took time to fish, though they'd had no luck.

My quiet empty camp was now hyperactive, filled with sound and motion. The steaming, smoking air shimmered and swirled above, the crackling grill fire mixed with the sounds of hissing grease and oils, the clicking of metal on metal, the solid clunk of knives on wooden cutting boards. Everyone had a role and got busy with it in a loosely orchestrated but workmanlike manner, like guys on a construction crew who appear to be making nothing but a mess until you see a structure begin to rise. Within the chaos, things were getting done and moving forward. No one was idle, except me. All I could do was mill around in genuine and audible astonishment at it all. They peppered me with offers of food.

"Hey, have some cheese and crackers."

"How 'bout some peanuts?"

"Want a pickle?"

"Got olives."

"You're *gonna* have one a these steaks."

One of the guys tending a gas stove poured oil and vinegar into a large frying pan which he placed on the burner. He cut up some tomatoes and onions and threw them in. He added salt, let it simmer for about a minute, and took it off the fire. He threw it all onto a plate and passed it around. Cheese and crackers were laid out. The duffel-size bag of peanuts was opened.

All I asked for was a Coke. After a few days of lukewarm water, it is something I crave and the first thing I go for when I finish a trip and hit the road. They didn't have any. So I had a couple of beers. I never bring alcohol on canoe trips but I couldn't pass up a cold carbonated drink.

They wanted to know about my trip. How had I fared alone against the wind? Had I seen any moose? They'd seen none (probably due to their never being on the river in the early morning or evening). They had seen three bald eagles, however, to my one. They didn't ask why I was out there alone. Instead, they joked about how much better off they'd be if they were away from each other. Male group humor—and much of male group conversation consists of attempts at humor—is filled with sarcasm, slights, and slurs, a constant and ornate verbal dance of mutual ridicule which indelicately carries the subtle message that, despite your ugliness, mental retardation, dismal career, unfortunate ethnic heritage, delinquent children, vile neighborhood, sexual deviance and inadequacy, and utter failure as a human being, you are still alright with us. This is the way my friends are. These guys were no different.

They hooted when I told them my job, immediately informing me of each others' depravities and need for immediate treatment. I told them they were all clearly far too sick for me to be of any help and would probably need immediate hospitalization with repeated treatments of electroshock therapy. They liked that.

We talked about canoe trips and I told them about some of mine. They loved the idea of being flown in rather than making that thirteen-hour drive from Massachusetts to Round Pond by way of St. Francis. They were eager to hear of the St. Croix and Moose River trips. I gave them names of shuttle drivers, river distances, driving distances from Massachusetts, and everything I could think of to help them choose and plan a trip. I loved being able to talk about it.

I asked them if they had seen the gear in the river today. Not only had they seen it, they knew all about how it got there. The story, I expect, is destined to spread up and down the Allagash Waterway and hang on there for a long time to come. It turned out we had crossed paths before. The men I had passed at midmorning out in the river "practicing rescue techniques" just before I encountered the debris were none other than these guys. What I hadn't seen were two old men, the owners of the cooler, paddle, gas can, etc., warming themselves around a fire at the campsite on shore. The canoe my pals had out in the water belonged to the daredevil duo. It had been damaged on the rocks. I actually *had* heard the words "duct tape." These guys had used it to repair a tear in the canoe and had been testing it for leaks when I passed.

The night before, at 10:00, two 80-year-old physicians had set out, in the *dark, against* the current, through a rock-strewn river at *low* water, in a motor-powered canoe, *drunk,* intending to fish at Round Pond in the morning. Their plans had gone awry when they crashed on rocks, tore their canoe, and lost their unsecured gear in the pitch black current. Luckily for them a campsite was near. They could see colored tents in the dark and were able to wade to them and wake up my new friends, who provided a fire to warm and dry them and shelter for the night. Otherwise, they'd have been forced to spend the cold night sitting wet on the riverside where hypothermia might have embraced them instead.

The sun had finally fallen behind the trees and the sherbet sky had lost its glow and deeply darkened. In the shade of the trees it was nearly night. Bedtime for me. I bid my camp mates adieu, telling them to stay up as late as they wanted and not to worry about noise, because I can sleep through anything, which is entirely untrue but I didn't want them to mind my going to bed early.

I took an empty gallon water bottle into the tent with me that night to use as a urinal so that I wouldn't have to leave the tent and subject myself to another ponkie attack. I settled in and read my Elmore Leonard. The guys retired pretty early, too. Despite the lure of fragrant drippings and the availability of unsecured food bags, we had no hairy visitors that night. I rose early to a sleeping camp. I packed quietly and left without eating, not wanting to take the time or disturb my guests. I was on the water at 5:45 A.M. During the night the sky had clouded over and it was not so cool as it had been the morning before. There was little fog. But the air was heavy. The sun rose drearily. I paddled under a dull pale flour-colored sky.

XVIII

THE FINAL EIGHT MILES TO ALLAGASH VILLAGE ARE A PRETTY STRAIGHT run. The river remained wide and shallow. Choosing channels held much of my attention. The sides of the river, though, had changed. The banks were high, sandy, and in places eroded and scooped out. Vegetation rarely reached the water and for the most part stayed well back, a wide layer of gravel, sand, and stone separating the green from the blue. The trees too were brutally scarred. All along the forest's edge the trees displayed trunks gouged by the ice, their bark ripped off, and the smooth bare inner wood exposed and turned gray. The line of damage was quite level and could easily be traced from tree to tree. It was a good ten to fifteen feet above the present waterline. The implications were at once inconceivable and inescapable. I had seen the effects of ice-out much farther upriver. I have a photograph of my first night's campsite. There is a tree a few feet from my tent with a scarred trunk which looks like it has been hit by a car. Down here on this lower stretch of the river, the marks of ice-out dominate. Here is where the ice begins to pile up and shoulder itself most roughly against its boundaries, changing the landscape around it. All the river's ice, which doesn't melt along the way, must pass through here. And here is where it begins to stall and back up. Up ahead at Allagash Village, the river makes two tight loops, bending right back on itself and then back again like a rounded letter N, within the space of a half mile before entering the St. John a few hundred yards farther on. The heaved and jagged shards clog up on the curves and jam up again when they try to enter the similarly ice-choked St. John. At ice-out, the two rivers meet with all the delicacy of a train wreck. White slabs of concrete-hard ice a foot thick and up to twenty feet square crunch and crash against each other, pushed and pulled from beneath by the relentless and gathering force of the spring flow. As it nears the village, unable to move freely forward, it spreads out, ripping into the river-banks and forest like a great annual glacier. The scarred trees are the wounded survivors. The dead are carried away with the ice.

Especially heavy winter snows and steady spring rains bring down a tidal wave of ice onto the village. In the spring of 1991, huge jams gathered on the Allagash and St. John Rivers, which hold the village between them in a V-shaped vise. On April 10 it tore down two modern steel and concrete bridges, grinding up the concrete and snapping and twisting the metal like pipe cleaners. Ten-million dollars worth of damage. The St. John River's bridge had been a 720-foot-long span. Lonna McBraierty was quoted the next day by the Associated Press.

"It rolled right back, just like opening a can of sardines. It snapped and cracked and made a lot of noise. It just kept rolling back until everything fell in. All the trees in front of my house are completely gone."

The ice jam had formed a dam which had held back the entire river. Once it broke, a wall of water was loosed, sweeping through the riverside homes. Chunks of ice were carried spinning and tumbling, stacking up in the yards and against houses, barns, and garages. Then it froze again. Twenty homes were encased in piles of ice higher than the roofs of some of the houses.

I asked Evelyn McBraierty about ice-out and she told me about 1991.

"A bunch of us went over St. John River to watch. We just had to see it." She shook her head as if recalling a foolishness of childhood. "Oh it's loud. You can hear it roar. Well, then the ice jammed up again and suddenly the water rose right up and around our knees before we know it. Seventeen of us had to stay the night over 'cross the river. We had no business being out there."

People like me come up here in the full summer and think we can achieve an understanding of the place and the people. But unless we have spent some winters here and seen the land and the water turned pure white and frozen solid, still and silent, encased in cold, we can't understand this place or these people. We cannot know the joy of the thaw, of the return of the long-gone warmth, and the moving water, the green buds, and the sound of birds. We are like visitors to a battlefield trying to know the feeling of war.

The first house came into view about 8:00 A.M., high above the water on the left or west bank. A quarter mile down was another; quiet, simple homes which had not yet come awake that Sunday morning. Signs facing the river advertised hunting camps, canoe rentals, and guide services. Straight ahead I could see the high embankment above which Route 161 skirts the river. The river makes its first loop turn there. A sea wall of large granite boulders covers the steep slope and serves as a bulwark against the Allagash's spring assault.

I finished at 8:30, at the empty landing before the Route 161 bridge. Mrs. McBraierty was sitting on her front porch. My truck wasn't due to be delivered for a couple of hours. I sat on the porch with her and heard about old-time Sundays, her father, who neither drank nor smoked, raised eleven children and lived to be 100 years old, about the logging days, the river, and her family. I called my wife. In May, a guy from Massachusetts canoeing down the St. John had drowned just half a mile from where I stood. He had capsized, hit the ice-cold water, and had a heart attack. I wanted to let her know I was fine and heading home.

CPSIA information can be obtained at www.ICGtesting.com
Printed in the USA
BVOW072249011211

277248BV00002B/96/P